OCR Cambridge Nationals in ICT

Level 1/2

Sonia Stuart
Brian Gillinder
Steve Cushing

Editors:
Penny Hill
Colin Harber Stuart

HODDER EDUCATION

The publisher would like to thank the following for permission to reproduce copyright material:

Photo credits
p.3 © Fotolia/vladgrin; **p.4** © Fotolia/michaeljung; **p.5** © Fotolia/WavebreakMediaMicro; **p.8** T © Maxim Kazmin/Fotolia, B © Dmitriy Chistoprudov/Fotolia, **p.9** T © Fotolia/Ben Chams, B © bloomua/Fotolia; **p.10** T © pizuttipics/Fotolia, B © Fotolia/Maksym Yemelyanov; **p.11** © Fotolia/Ammentorp; **p.14** T © Ingram Publishing Limited, B © Inclusive Technology; **p.15** T–B © anubis3211/Fotolia, © Siede Preis/Photodisc/Getty Images, © Werner Stoffberg/iStockphoto, © Dmitry Terentjev/Fotolia, © Lusoimages/Fotolia; **p.16** T–B © Siede Preis/Photodisc/Getty Images, © Stephen Coburn/Fotolia, © Gleam/Fotolia, © Evgeny Tyzhinov/Fotolia, © iStockphoto/bleex; **p.17** T–B © Steve Connolly, © BMPix/iStockphoto, © Jakub Semeniuk/iStockphoto; **p.18** T © Viktor Gmyria/Fotolia, B © Helix/Fotolia; **p.19** T–B © Greg Nicholas/iStockphoto, © Mohamed Saber/Fotolia, © Andrey Turchaninov/iStockphoto, © iStockphoto/Amanda Rohde; **p.20** © Jerome Dancette/Fotolia; **p.21** T–B © iStockphoto/Oleksiy Mark, © brentmelissa/iStockphoto, © Xuejun li/Fotolia; **p.23** T–B © mbongo/Fotolia, © Fotolia/Scanrail, © Norman Chan/iStockphoto; **p.24** T © Fotolia/imageteam, B © Stefano Maccari/Fotolia; **p.26** T © Origin Instruments Corporation, B © techno-vision.co.uk; **p.36** © Picsclamation!/Alamy; **p.38** © Jeff Morgan 13/Alamy; **p.39** © NetPics/Alamy; **p.40** © incamerastock/Alamy; **p.41** © Michael Kemp/Alamy; **p.46** T © pizmovka/Fotolia, B © Martin Shields/Science Photo Library; **p.49** L & R © Hodder Education; **p.50** T © rangizzz/Fotolia, B © Albert Lozano-Nieto/Fotolia; **p.51** © Chris Pearsall/Alamy; **p.63** © Fotolia/Andrea Danti; **p.64** T © NetPics/Alamy; B © Roy Wylam/Alamy; **p.65** T © Fotolia/KarSol, B © D. Hurst/Alamy; **p.67** © Yong Hian Lim/Fotolia; **p.73** © Roman Ivaschenko/Fotolia; **p.74** © Akhilesh Sharma/Fotolia; **p.75** © Fotolia/ashumskiy; **p.76** T © Fotolia/apops, B © Suprijono Suharjoto/Fotolia; **p.86** © Ian Dagnall/Alamy; **p.95** © Chris Rout/Alamy; **p.99** © Fotolia/Pavel Ignatov; **p.102** © Fotolia/eteimaging; **p.103** © Fotolia/martin33; **p.119** © Fotolia/alphaspirit; **p.120** © Fotolia/pressmaster; **p.124** © Chloe Johnson/Alamy; **p.131** © Vicki Reid/iStockphoto; **p.147** © kristian sekulic/iStockphoto; **p.148** © Sean Locke/iStockphoto; **p.166** © Thinkstock Images; **p.169** © Fotolia/Iakov Kalinin; **p.170** © Fotolia/Jacek Chabraszewski

© Microsoft product screenshots reprinted with permission from Microsoft Corporation.

Although every effort has been made to ensure that website addresses are correct at time of going to press, Hodder Education cannot be held responsible for the content of any website mentioned. It is sometimes possible to find a relocated web page by typing in the address of the home page for a website in the URL window of your browser.

Orders: please contact Bookpoint Ltd, 130 Milton Park, Abingdon, Oxon OX14 4SB.
Telephone: (44) 01235 827720. Fax: (44) 01235 400454. Lines are open 9.00–17.00, Monday to Saturday, with a 24-hour message answering service. Visit our website at www.hoddereducation.co.uk

© Sonia Stuart, Brian Gillinder and Steve Cushing 2012

First published in 2012 by
Hodder Education
An Hachette UK Company,
338 Euston Road
London NW1 3BH

Impression number	5	4	3	2
Year	2016	2015	2014	2013

Cover photo © HaywireMedia – Fotolia
Illustrations by GreenGate Publishing Services
Typeset in Horley Old Style by GreenGate Publishing Services, Tonbridge, Kent.
Printed in Dubai
A catalogue record for this title is available from the British Library.

ISBN 978 1 444 176537

Contents

Unit 1
Understanding computer systems

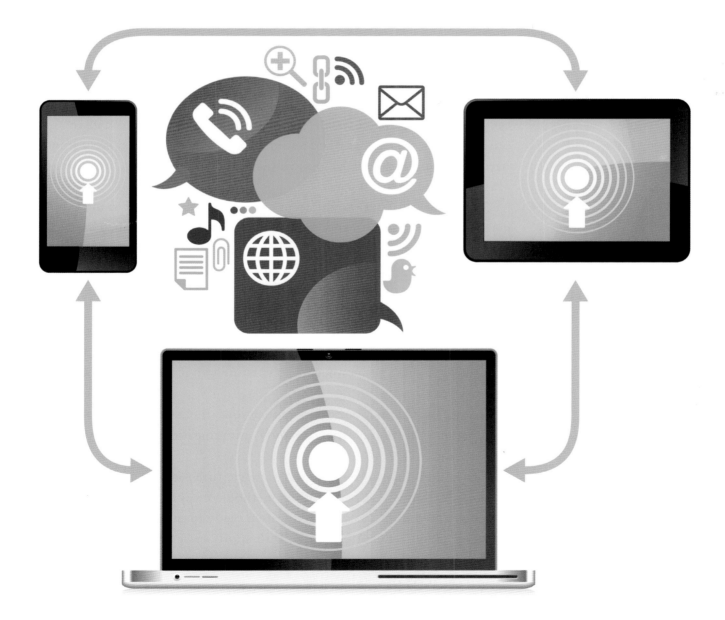

► *What you will learn*

- How ICT can be used to meet business needs.
- The features and uses of a range of computing devices that are commonly used in business.
- How desktop and portable computing devices, such as laptops, netbooks, tablets and smartphones, are used by people in business.
- Why a particular type of computing device is suitable, or not, for use in business tasks.

Introduction

The features and typical uses of computing devices are shown in tables to make it easy for you to see how they might be used in business. The advantages and disadvantages of each are clearly shown so that they are easy for you to learn in readiness for the written examination.

As you work through Unit 1 of the book you will read how costs, availability, user needs and the need for data security affect the choice of computer systems used in business and by employees of organisations.

You will learn about common input devices including mice and keyboards, webcams, touch screens, readers for bar codes and magnetic stripes, and chip and pin devices, and about specialist input devices such as adapted keyboards for visually disabled people. Common output devices including monitors, printers and speakers, and more specialised devices such as digital projectors and activators are also covered.

Storage devices and their uses are explained, to help you gain a better understanding of the devices needed to store files and data in business. The features of fixed and portable storage devices, including hard disks, solid state disks, optical disks and cloud storage, are shown along with their typical uses.

You will learn about the different software that is needed to make computing devices work and allow users to carry out tasks such as writing letters, storing and manipulating data, and communicating with others. You will also learn how software may be set up and configured to meet different needs such as working when travelling, working from home or those of people with physical impairments.

The use of peripherals that can be connected to a computer device by wired and wireless methods is explained, and you will find out how computing devices are connected to existing wireless networks using security keys.

The use of ICT in monitoring applications, including GPS location tracking, monitoring internet use and communications, is also described.

You will read about the design of data capture forms including automated, online and paper-based methods of capturing data so that it can be entered into a computer system ready for use. You will learn how to design data capture forms, with appropriate data validation methods, and gain knowledge of how information can be coded for use in a spreadsheet or database.

You will find out how data can be stored in different file formats and kept secure, and how it can be transferred securely. You should also use the information provided to find out how to keep your own data safe and secure using backups and archives. This will provide you with an insight into how businesses ensure that their data is not lost or misused, and about the factors that affect how methods of backup and disaster recovery are chosen. Data loss can be disastrous – and very embarrassing – for a business so here you can read about the implications and consequences to a business of losing information such as customer details and how businesses can deal with threats to the security of their data.

This unit also covers how ICT can be used to support business working practices. Communications such as VoIP (Voice over Internet Protocol) and videoconferencing are explained to provide you with an understanding of how businesses use modern communication methods to keep in contact with employees and those working away from the office. Organising work schedules with diary management software, the creation of documents and collaboration in authoring and editing of documents are all described and explained.

Legal, ethical and security issues that affect the use of computers are important to business. You will learn how current legislation applies to the use of computers, and about the moral and ethical issues that businesses have to deal with as a result of using computers.

Key words are listed throughout the unit, so you can pick out some of the most important facts easily when revising. Definitions for all the keywords are given in the glossary at the back of the book.

The examination

Hints and tips have been included in this book. These will help you to focus on what the examiner will be looking for when they are assessing your answers to the examination questions.

A number of activities are suggested throughout the unit, and these are provided to expand on the information shown in the book, to help you to learn how to find information for yourself and to apply your knowledge.

To prepare yourself for the written examination, you should work through the exam-type questions, using the information in the text and the tables to answer the questions as carefully and concisely as you can. When answering the questions, try not to write too much – or too little – and read your answers to yourself when you have finished each question to check that you have actually answered it, included all the required information and that everything makes sense! If it doesn't make sense to you, it won't make sense to an examiner.

1 How ICT can be used to meet business needs

▶ **Specification coverage**

Desktop and portable devices:
- Laptops
- Netbooks
- Tablets
- Smartphones

▶ **What you will learn**

The features of desktop and portable devices and how they are used.

Introduction

Schools, colleges and universities use IT to:
- advertise courses and staff vacancies
- provide access to information about themselves and for teaching and learning
- collect data, for example tracking the performance of students and teachers
- carry out administration, for example making timetables, writing letters and reports to parents/students
- support the teaching and learning of students, for example using computers in subjects such as art, design and music.

Businesses and organisations such as estate agents and leisure centres use IT to:
- sell services to their customers
- plan and monitor the finances of the business
- communicate between members of staff
- communicate with customers.

Central and local government use IT to allow citizens to access information about government services via the internet. Access to government services using IT allows citizens to:
- complete and file tax forms online and to make tax payments
- complete and confirm entries in an electoral register so that they can vote in elections
- apply for official documents such as driving licences, passports and identification documents
- take part in government by signing online petitions and questionnaires, and lobbying politicians.

Governments also use IT to make information available to the population via websites and emails as well as in the creation and publication of documents.

Employees use IT to carry out their work. For example, estate agent employees use IT in their offices to store details of properties and clients, and when they are out and about to show prospective buyers details of houses for sale or rent.

Central and local government employees use IT in their offices, when out on government business, and in public libraries and leisure centres.

Customers can use IT to:

- research companies that they might wish to buy items from
- contact companies
- place and pay for orders
- track orders
- provide feedback to the company about what they think of their products and service.

Case study: Leisure centre

A leisure centre offers a wide range of facilities including a sports hall where visitors can take part in a variety of sports. Many clubs including abseiling, canoeing, fencing and aikido are also held in the sports hall. There is also a health suite, sauna and steam room, gym and swimming pool.

The centre employs a number of trainers and coaches who support visitors in their training and use of the facilities, as well as offering lessons in many sporting skills. The trainers and coaches use laptops and smartphones to keep in contact with other staff and to access visitor details and training records.

The centre encourages visitors with disabilities so its **computer systems** and equipment have been designed and installed in such a way that disabled persons can use them.

Computers are used to:

- control the temperature of pools and rooms
- control lifts and hoists to enable disabled persons to access pools and facilities more easily
- control automatic door opening and closing, or respond to specially designed door locks or access codes
- provide access to services by disabled people.

Key word

Computer systems

Case study: Estate agent

A typical independent estate agent sells properties in the local area and has a large commercial property department.

The company also represents the builders of various new housing estates in the area and the re-selling of houses as people move on. With large numbers of the local population commuting to neighbouring towns there is often a thriving market in the agent's property rental and lettings division.

The company can also offer added services including conveyancing, financial advice, mortgage broking and household insurance broking.

IT and computer devices are used in many ways by staff working for estate agents. For example:

- Word processing and desktop publishing software (DTP software) is used to write advertising reports for houses for sale.
- Staff use spreadsheets for finances, databases for storing client details, email for communications and web browsers for viewing web pages.
- Digital cameras (or the cameras in smartphones) are used to take digital images to advertise houses for sale or rent.
- Digital cameras (or the cameras in smartphones) are used to take digital images of the contents of houses for rent so that a record can be made of what is in the house when people move into it. This helps in checking the condition of the property and contents when the people move out.
- Giving the location and directions to houses for sale or rent using the navigation software or global positioning system (GPS) in smartphones or by searching on the internet on smartphones or laptops.
- Dedicated satellite navigation systems using GPS can be used to navigate to and from houses for sale or rent.

Computing devices and their use/purpose in businesses

Desktop and portable computer systems are used by employers and employees in nearly every business or organisation.

Key word

Desktop computer

Desktop computer systems are used in almost any place that people work and need to access and use information. For example:

- offices
- shops
- warehouses
- libraries, health and leisure centres.

Modern mobile communication systems allow workers to take portable devices away from the workplace and to access the same information that would be available in their actual workplace. There is no longer any real need for many workers to be physically in a workplace as they can quite easily work remotely, for example when working from home.

Desktop computer systems

Desktop computer systems are usually found in the offices where employees work. These systems are quite large and heavy, and are not suitable for use when moving from place to place. While some employees prefer not to share their computers, these can be shared amongst employees who work at different times. This is known as 'hot-desking'.

To make sure that employees do not see, or interfere with, each other's work and files when moving around an office or hot-desking, each employee may be given their own login and password. When an employee logs in using their unique username (user ID), the computer system asks for a password that, if it is correctly entered, will allow the employee to access the system but only to his or her files and authorised areas. The password identifies the employee to the system and is used by the system as a security check to try and make sure that it is the actual employee who is trying to log in.

Key word

Portable computer

Portable computer systems

Portable computers, such as laptops, tablets, netbooks and smartphones, are personal computers designed for mobile use and are not permanently placed on a desk. These systems are for use when travelling from place to place and the user wishes to carry a computing device to communicate with others and to access files and data while away from their usual place of work. Since some portable computers can do most, if not all of the tasks required in business, portable computers are often used instead of desktop computers even if the user does not travel around.

Features of desktop and portable computer systems

Computing system	Features	Purpose or typical use
Desktop computers	Kept in one place, quite large and difficult to move from place to place. Although the main components can be in a box unit, there are usually separate input and output devices such as the keyboard, monitor and mouse. Connection to a network is usually by wire but can be by using wireless technology. Some desktop computers have the main components built into the monitor casing. This type of computer system is usually powered from the mains electricity and not batteries. Desktop computers should be safely placed on a suitable surface such as a desk and can be secured to a solidly fixed bracket so they are difficult to steal.	Office-based tasks, such as: ● writing letters ● reports ● memos ● using spreadsheets and databases ● creating presentations. They can also be used for: ● browsing the internet using web browsers ● creating web pages and websites ● audio and video editing.
Laptops	Laptops are lighter in weight than desktop computers so can be carried from place to place or used while travelling, for example on trains and aircraft. Input and output devices such as keyboard, monitor and pointing device are built in. A separate mouse is often used instead of the in-built pointing device as some people find these unsuitable. Optical storage devices are usually built in. This type of computer system can be powered from the mains electricity and by batteries. Using batteries allows the laptop to be moved around easily. Laptops are easily damaged while being moved and are easy to steal. Connection to a network is usually wireless but can be by wire.	An internet connection allows the user to carry out office-based tasks, such as those for desktop computers, and most of the other tasks, while away from a fixed office location and when travelling. Laptops are very useful for: ● sending and receiving emails ● **instant messaging** ● live web chat. Laptops allow users to carry out tasks using applications that require larger memory capacity than found in netbooks or smartphones. Users can use laptops to create documents with DTP software, edit video or audio, and create presentations as easily as if using a desktop computer but without being confined to one place. Laptops allow the user to be mobile.

Key word

Instant messaging

Computing system	Features	Purpose or typical use
Netbooks	Netbooks are smaller and even lighter in weight than laptops, and are easily carried or used while travelling, for example on trains and aircraft. Input and output devices such as keyboard, monitor and pointing device are built in. A separate mouse is often used because the area containing the pointing device can be quite small and hard to use. Netbooks usually have a lower specification than laptop or desktop computers. Their keyboards can be difficult to use as they are small. A separate optical drive for CDs and DVDs is needed because, to keep size and weight to a minimum, most netbooks do not have them built in. The processing power and memory capacity of netbooks is less than in laptops so software applications that need fast processors and a lot of memory run slower or even not at all. This type of computer system can be powered from the mains electricity and by batteries. Using batteries allows the netbook to be moved around easily. Storage of data can be on an internal hard disk drive or a solid-state disk drive. Connection to networks is usually wireless but can be by wire.	An internet connection allows the user to carry out office-based tasks, such as those for desktop and laptop computers, and most of the other tasks, while away from the office and when travelling. The lower specification of netbooks means that tasks take longer and some cannot be done at all. While out of the office, netbooks are most useful for: • sending and receiving emails • instant messaging • live web chat • browsing the internet.
Tablet computers	Tablet computers are usually even smaller than laptops or netbooks as they often have no physical keyboard or pointing device at all. The keyboard is on-screen and pointing is done with the fingers on-screen. There is a touch screen that, as well as displaying the screen content, can: • display an on-screen keyboard for typing • respond to touch gestures such as swiping or pinching objects to move or resize the objects on screen • run an application that will take over the whole screen and hide all other applications that may be in use at the same time. Storage of data can be on a solid-state disk drive but some tablet computers have a hard disk drive. This type of computer system is powered by batteries. Using batteries allows the user to move around easily while using the device.	Most office tasks can be done on tablet computers but users find this awkward or difficult as they are not used to the different way the software works on tablet computers. With increasing familiarity with the software and performance of tablet computers, these tasks should become easier in time. While out of the office, tablet computers are most useful for: • sending and receiving emails • instant messaging • live web chat • browsing the internet • viewing photographs or images.

Computing system	Features	Purpose or typical use
Smartphones	A smartphone is a portable or mobile computer system that combines: ● a mobile telephone used for voice conversations and text messaging ● a personal digital assistant (PDA) with features such as a diary and calendar, and for managing personal information ● web browser ● media player for viewing video and listening to music ● connections to the mobile phone network and to the internet via the phone network or a wireless network ● a digital camera ● a GPS system ● a touch screen for input and output ● the ability to run applications (apps). Storage of data is on a solid-state flash memory card. These devices are powered by batteries. Using batteries allows the user to move around easily while using the smartphone. Smartphone technology is being continually improved so more and more business-related apps are becoming available that allow office tasks to be carried out on these devices. Also, apps allow users to exchange data between their smartphone and company servers so they can be kept up to date with all the information they require.	Used for keeping in contact with fellow workers and friends while on the move. Typical uses include: ● telephone conversations with friends and colleagues ● keeping personal and business diaries ● using applications (apps) for getting directions, finding locations and organising photographs ● sending and receiving emails ● sending and receiving text messages ● web browsing.

Activity

Look on the internet and choose any one of the latest laptops and one of the latest smartphone models.

Copy and complete the following table to show the features of your chosen devices:

	Laptop	Smartphone
Manufacturer		
Model		
Cost		
Size of screen		
Processor speed		
Amount of memory installed		
Storage devices installed		
Type of keyboard		
Number of USB ports		
Wi-Fi?		
Cable network connection?		
Bluetooth® available?		

Choose one of the two devices and create an advertisement showing and explaining the features that might persuade a business person to use it when working remotely.

Advantages and disadvantages of the different types of computer systems

Type of computer system	Advantages	Disadvantages
Desktop	<ul><li>Usually high performance specification so can carry out all office tasks.</li><li>Easy to replace or upgrade components.</li><li>Position of monitor can be adjusted for comfort of use and to reduce potential health problems.</li><li>Screen size can be very large.</li></ul>	<ul><li>Can take up a lot of space.</li><li>Fixed in one location.</li></ul>
Laptop	<ul><li>Portable because they are small, light in weight and the monitor, pointing device and keyboard are built in.</li><li>Can run from battery power so can be used away from office locations.</li></ul>	<ul><li>More easily damaged or stolen than desktops.</li><li>More difficult to repair or upgrade as all components are built in.</li><li>Battery life can be limited so restricting mobile use.</li><li>Can be easily lost or stolen.</li><li>Care needs to be taken to keep data secure and safe.</li></ul>
Netbook	<ul><li>Very portable because they are much smaller, lighter in weight and the monitor, pointing device and keyboard are built in.</li><li>Can run longer from battery power so can be used away from office locations.</li></ul>	<ul><li>Usually lower specification than other computer types so tasks are slower or more difficult.</li><li>As with laptops, netbooks are more easily damaged or stolen than desktops and are more difficult to repair or upgrade as all components are built in.</li><li>Do not have optical drives so cannot use CDs or DVDs without adding an external drive.</li><li>Can be easily lost or stolen.</li><li>Care needs to be taken to keep data secure and safe.</li></ul>
Tablet	<ul><li>Very light and thin so are highly portable for mobile use.</li><li>Can support a variety of apps that provide entertainment, communication and **social networking**, etc.</li></ul>	<ul><li>Cannot easily be used to carry out many office tasks, in terms of creating and editing files, due to touch screen technology.</li><li>Typing on a touch screen is a different experience from typing on a conventional keyboard but some people can type just as fast using a touch screen.</li></ul>

Type of computer system	Advantages	Disadvantages
Tablet		• Different keyboard layouts (for example, split keyboards for use by thumbs) can be used to make typing easier on screen. • More care needs to be taken to keep data secure and safe. • Limited connectivity to external devices such as flash drives for some models.
Smartphone	• Small and light so very portable. • Ideal for mobile communication with colleagues, viewing information, and sending and receiving emails while away from the office. • Can also be used for entertainment and web browsing.	• Cannot carry out many office tasks. • Can be too small for easy typing and viewing of complex documents. • Can be easily lost or stolen. • More care needs to be taken to keep data secure and safe.

Hints and tips

You must ensure that you keep up to date with the features of desktop computers and portable computers such as laptops and smartphones. Smartphones are really small computers and are being used more and more by people to keep in contact with friends and colleagues. It is important that you make sure that you know how the features help workers in their jobs. Exam questions will ask you explain how these features can be useful in specific business situations.

Exam-type questions

1 Explain **one** reason why a trainer in a leisure centre would prefer to use a tablet rather than a desktop computer. [2 marks]

2 Explain why an office worker would prefer to use a desktop computer rather than a tablet for typing letters. [4 marks]

3 Describe **three** ways that a sales person working for an estate agent would use a smartphone to keep in contact with his office staff. [6 marks]

What you will learn

The features of input devices and how they are used.

Input, output, storage and connectivity devices

Input devices

Input devices all have the same purpose – to enable the user to enter or input data so that instructions or commands can be given to the computer.

Case study: Leisure centre

A leisure centre needs a variety of input devices so that its staff can enter details of visitors, take bookings, type letters, create memos and reports, and so that the details on visitors' credit or debit cards can be read so that the visitor can pay for the use of the facilities or for membership fees. Visitors to the leisure centre website need input devices on their own computers so that they can enter information into, for example, an online form for making a booking to use the facilities such as a badminton court.

The staff of an estate agent would use input devices to enter the details of their clients who were buying or selling property, renting out property or renting houses in which to live, as well as the details of the properties themselves. Cameras would be used to take photographs of the outside and inside of properties when advertising a property for sale or to record the contents, such as chairs, tables, beds and kitchen appliances, when it is rented out.

Some input devices and their uses are shown in the following table:

Input device	Features	Purpose	Typical use in the leisure centre and estate agent
Keyboard	Keys labelled with characters and set out in a pattern so that each is easy to reach by fingers.	Entering characters such as letters, punctuation marks, numbers and symbols.	• Typing letters. • Creating memos and reports. • Entering visitor data into spreadsheets and databases. • Entering commands into a computer.
Specialist keyboards	Keys labelled with the same characters as an 'ordinary' keyboard, but set out in a different pattern or with the raised marks of Braille so that visually impaired people can feel the keys.	Entering characters. Specialist keyboards can be designed for disabled users. For example, Braille keyboards for the visually impaired and engineering keyboards for specialised character entry.	A visually impaired receptionist or member might use a Braille keyboard to enter their details.

Input device	Features	Purpose	Typical use in the leisure centre and estate agent
Mouse	A mouse can be used to move a pointer on screen and has one or more buttons that can be clicked to select items on screen.	Used to move pointer on screen and select choice from a menu.	Choosing items from an onscreen menu and selecting using a click.
Microphone	A microphone converts sounds to electrical signals that can be digitised for use in computer systems.	Capturing sounds.	Talking on a mobile phone or when using video-conferencing or audio chat.
Key pad	Keys labelled with characters as with an 'ordinary' keyboard, but with fewer keys – often only numbers and a few other characters such as * and #.	Entering characters or commands.	Entering the price or cost of an item.
Touch pad	A touch sensitive panel that responds to the fingers' movements. By moving a finger over the surface, it can be used to move a pointer on screen and tapping can act as a mouse click.	Translating the position and movement of a person's fingers into movement on screen.	Used on a laptop instead of a mouse to allow a user to choose from an onscreen menu and to select using a tap of the finger.
Remote controls	These can be wired or use wireless such as infrared to send command signals to devices including TVs or wheelchairs.	Inputting commands or instructions into computer systems or equipment. Remote controls can be used with TVs and DVD players but also with training equipment in leisure centres.	Used to control training equipment or facilities in a leisure centre.

Input device	Features	Purpose	Typical use in the leisure centre and estate agent
Scanner	These use reflected light from documents or photographs to capture their image. Scans can be made using different sizes and resolutions, and printed documents can be converted to text for use in a word processor.	Capturing images or documents from printed paper copies.	Capturing printed documents for use in a word processor or capturing images for use in documents such as membership cards.
Bar code reader or scanner	The lines or matrix of a bar code are scanned and converted for input into a computer system.	Capturing a bar code made up of lines or a matrix of black modules arranged in a square on white background.	The captured bar code is used to look up the details of the item in a database.
Chip and PIN reader	The reader has a slot for the card so that the chip can be read, a magnetic stripe reader for use if the chip cannot be read (or a card has no chip), and a keypad for entering the PIN.	Reading the data from a chip and allowing the entering of characters.	When paying for goods using a credit or debit card, the details are read from the card and checked using the PIN entered by the purchaser.
Magnetic stripe reader	The reader reads the data from a magnetic stripe when it is 'swiped' through a slot in the reader.	Reading the data from a magnetic stripe.	A membership card for a leisure centre might have a magnetic stripe holding details about the member. When paying for goods using a credit or debit card, the details are read from the magnetic stripe if the card has no chip or the chip cannot be read.
MIDI	Connects musical instruments to computer systems using a special interface.	Can be used for storing and transmitting music data.	Used for connecting musical instruments to a computer for transmitting music data to and from the musical instruments.

Input device	Features	Purpose	Typical use in the leisure centre and estate agent
Touch screen	A touch screen is a visual display unit that has a touch sensitive layer that responds to movements of a finger or stylus.	Entering characters or commands by selecting an image or other item on screen to enable data to be entered in situations where a separate keyboard is not suitable (for example, on small portable devices) or to enable the user to directly control objects displayed on the screen (for example, by dragging objects). This is also an output device.	Used in smartphones and tablet computers to detect finger touches and movements on a screen.
Sensors	Sensors convert physical parameters such as light into electrical signals.	To measure physical parameters such as temperature, pressure and light. Also to measure body temperature and heart rate.	Used to measure the temperature or light levels of a sports hall, swimming pool or offices so that the measurements can be used to control a heating/air-conditioning system, or filtration and pumping system for the pool. Sensors can also be used to detect the presence of people at a door or to trigger a security system.
Camera	Light sensitive receptors convert light into electrical signals that are digitised so that they can be stored as digital images by computer systems.	To capture images. Can be used for still or moving (video) images.	Used to take the photograph of a new member, to capture video of sports performances, or for video surveillance in CCTV.

Hints and tips

Smartphones and tablet computers use touch screens to allow the user to input commands and data, and to make choices. Exam questions will ask you how a worker would make use of a touch screen and other input devices when doing their work.

Exam-type questions

1 Identify **three** input devices that could be used with a desktop computer and give **one** use for each. [6 marks]

2 Describe how a touch screen on a smartphone can be used to display and view a photograph stored in its memory. [4 marks]

3 Describe how a photograph of a new member could be captured by a receptionist at a leisure centre so that it could be input into a database and used on a membership card. [3 marks]

▶ Specification coverage

Output devices:
- Monitors/screens
- Printers and plotters
- Speakers and head/ earphones
- Digital or data projectors
- Plotters
- Actuators

▶ What you will learn

The features of output devices and how they are used.

Output devices

Output devices also take many forms but all have the same purpose – to show the results to the user of any tasks and processing that the computer has performed.

Case studies

A leisure centre needs a variety of output devices so that its staff can view or print the details of visitors and bookings, send out letters, memos and reports, and monitor the activities of visitors as they perform.

The staff of an estate agent would use output devices to view or print details of their clients and any photographs of the contents of a rented property when, for instance, the person is leaving the property.

Some output devices and their uses are shown in the following table:

Output device	Purpose	Typical use in a business
Monitor	Used to show results from processing.	Displaying characters as they are typed, video as it is played, replaying sports performances or watching CCTV images.
Touch screen	This is a type of monitor and has the same purpose as any other monitor. Touch screens are also input devices so have a dual function that is useful in small devices such as smartphones.	A user of a smartphone will use a touch screen just like monitor. On a smartphone the screen would be much smaller than a monitor attached to a desktop computer and also act as an input device due to its touch sensitivity.

Output device	Purpose	Typical use in a business
Printer	Produces hard copy of results of processing.	Printing letters, images, photographs, membership cards or passes, and receipts. Laser and inkjet printers are commonly used. Laser printers can print large quantities of high-quality copies in a short time and can have lower running costs in offices. Inkjet printers can produce high-quality colour prints but are usually slower to print and have higher running costs.
Speaker, earphones, headphones	Produce sounds.	Allows user to hear audio files, music, movie soundtracks, the voices of other people in an audio or video conference.
Data or digital projector	Project and enlarge a computer display on to a screen for viewing by an audience of several people.	Showing presentations to members and staff.
Plotter	Printing large drawings.	These are used for printing designs and plans, for example in engineering companies or architects.

Hints and tips

You should be able to compare the features of each device and decide which one is best for a particular task. For example, a laser printer can print large numbers of copies very quickly.

Activity

Use the internet to find out about specialised hardware and software that can help people with the following disabilities to use computers:
- Partially sighted people and people who cannot see at all.
- Physically disabled people who cannot use their arms and hands.
- People with hearing difficulties.

Exam-type questions

1 Identify **three** output devices that could be used by a receptionist at a leisure centre and give **one** use for each. [6 marks]

2 Why would a receptionist use a laser printer instead of an inkjet printer to print notices of maintenance works to hand out to all visitors and members as they arrive? [2 marks]

Storage devices

Storage devices are used to store the files of data that a user wants to keep. Files of data may be letters, images, photographs, spreadsheet or database files, or any data that has to be kept after the computer is switched off, or when the user has moved on to another task and wants to save the data for later use.

Case studies

A leisure centre needs a storage device so that its staff can save the details of visitors, any bookings, letters, memos and reports that they have produced, and to store the training records and any readings taken from visitors while they were performing. Records of the use of facilities, finances and staff information would also have to be kept and stored.

The staff of an estate agent would use storage devices to save details of their clients and photographs of the contents of a rented property to be referred to when, for instance, the person is leaving the property. Details of appointments for viewing properties, meetings with clients and electronic diaries would also be kept on a computer system. Financial and staff employment records would also have to be stored.

Some storage devices, features and uses are shown in the following table:

Storage device	Features	Typical use in a business
Hard disk drive using magnetic disks	A hard disk drive uses magnetic disks for storing software and data in files. The disks are circular and spin at high speeds while drive heads read and write the data. This makes the disks susceptible to dirt and damage if moved suddenly. The files can be read, edited, re-written or deleted. Hard disks can store huge amounts of data.	Uses include: ● storage of the operating system ● storage of the files and data not in use at the time ● storage of data, files and software when the computer is turned off ● storing a database of the details of members.

Storage device	Features	Typical use in a business
Solid-state drive	A solid-state drive uses **flash memory** to store software and data in files. There are no moving parts in solid state drives which makes them faster and more reliable than magnetic hard disk drives and they are often found in portable computers such as netbooks and tablet computers. Solid-state drives are faster in use than hard disk drives. They can store large amounts of data but not as much as hard disk drives.	Uses include: ● storage of the operating system ● storage of the files and data not in use at the time ● storage of data, files and software when the computer is turned off.
Optical device	An optical drive uses **optical media** such as CDs and DVDs to store software and data in files. The files can be read, edited, re-written or deleted only if CDR/RWs or DVD-R/RWs are used. Data stored on CDROMS and DVD-ROMs can be read but cannot be altered. Blu-ray disks are large capacity optical disks and can store very large amounts of data.	Uses include: ● storage of files or data that have to be moved to another computer ● storage software for installation on a computer ● storage of data, files and software in backups or archives. Businesses may use writable or re-writable CDs and DVDs for storing backups and archives.
Flash memory devices	Small memory sticks contain flash memory and are used in **USB** ports. They are used to store data and files for transfer to other computers or for taking away from, or back to, the office. Similar devices are used in cameras and phones as memory cards.	Typical uses include saving a file on to a memory stick (flash memory device), saving images in cameras or **contact** details in a phone.
Cloud storage	Very large data storage capacity facilities made available online so the data can be accessed remotely using a web interface.	Used to store files that are shared between all staff.

Activity

1 Find out what units are used to describe the capacity of storage devices.

2 Find out, and write down, the capacity of one of each of these storage devices:
   i) CD
   ii) DVD
   iii) Blu-ray disk
   iv) USB memory stick costing under £10
   v) USB memory stick costing between £10 and £30
   vi) an external hard disk costing around £100
   vii) a solid-state disk costing around £200.

Hints and tips

You should be able to compare the features of the storage devices to explain how each is suitable, or not suitable, for a particular task. For example, a USB flash memory stick is useful for transferring documents between computers but is easily lost.

Solid-state drives are suitable for devices such as portable computers because they are smaller and less easily damaged by movement than magnetic hard disks.

Exam-type questions

1 Describe **two** features of a USB memory stick that make it suitable for transferring files between computers.   [4 marks]

2 Explain **two** reasons why an estate agent might decide to store its files using cloud storage rather than on its own file servers.   [4 marks]

3 Explain **one** advantage of using writable DVDs instead of writable CDs for storing data.   [2 marks]

► *Specification coverage*

Connectivity devices:
■ network devices

► *What you will learn*

The features of connectivity devices and how they are used.

Connectivity devices

Connectivity devices are used to connect computer systems together. Some devices are built into computers to connect a computer to a **network** or to the internet while some are used to connect networks together or into the internet.

Key words

Network
Ethernet

Case studies

A leisure centre would have a computer network so that all its desktop and laptop computers can have access to customer details and to any other useful information that might be wanted by its staff when carrying out their duties.

An estate agent would also have a computer network connecting its desktop and laptop computers so that details of the buyers and sellers of property, or properties for sale or rent, can be shared between office staff, the property sales people and those who visit rented properties.

Some connectivity devices that may be needed for the leisure centre network, their purpose and typical uses are shown in the following table:

Connectivity device	Purpose	Typical use in a business
Network card (NIC)	Connecting a computer to a network using a cable.	Connecting a desktop PC to a company network using an **ethernet** cable.
Wireless NIC	Connecting a computer to a network using radio waves.	Connecting a laptop or netbook to a company network or to the internet using Wi-Fi. Tablet computers use wireless NICs to connect as they normally do not have a socket for a cable connection. Wireless cards are also in smartphones so they can connect to a network using Wi-Fi.
Router	Directs network traffic to the correct computer or device.	These are used to connect different networks together and to the internet. These are sometimes called 'modems' in homes but this is not the correct term – a modem converts analogue to digital signals (or vice versa) and there is no need for this when using broadband connections. The correct term is 'router'.

Connectivity device	Purpose	Typical use in a business
Switch 	Allows many computers or devices to connect to a network.	These are used in larger networks to connect devices.
Modem	Converts analogue signals to and from digital signals so that ordinary telephone lines can be used to connect to the internet.	These connect to the internet by a 'dial up' connection using ordinary telephone lines.
Wireless access point (WAP)	To connect devices to a network using wireless/ Wi-Fi.	A WAP is used to allow devices to use Wi-Fi to connect into an existing network.

Key word

Wireless access point (WAP)

Hints and tips

You should make sure that you know how businesses make use of each of the networking devices to connect their computers and to share data between their employees.

Exam-type questions

1 State **two** advantages of using a laptop with a wireless rather than a wired connection to the internet. [2 marks]

2 State **two** disadvantages of using a laptop with a wireless rather than a wired connection to the internet. [2 marks]

3 Why are several wireless access points needed in a leisure centre? [2 marks]

▶ Specification coverage

Factors that affect the choice of system:
- Cost
- Availability
- User needs
- Data security

Choosing a system

Computer systems in business situations have to be suitable for the tasks required of them, meet the needs of the people who use them, be configured to keep data secure, and be ready for use when required.

Expensive machines designed for gaming or video editing are not required and computers used in a business environment are designed

What you will learn

How the choice of a computer system by a business can be affected by various factors.

Key words

Resolution
Processor
Data security

Specification coverage

- Typical office configurations
- Customised systems for specified needs:
  - Physical impairment (sight, hearing, movement)
  - Remote working

What you will learn

How typical office systems can be configured and customised.

Key words

Operating system
Application

to be suitable without costing too much to buy or maintain. There is no need for most businesses to have very large high-**resolution** monitors or top of the range, high-speed **processors** unless the business is dealing with large graphics or video files.

Business computers must be capable of running office applications at a reasonable speed, store data safely and securely, and have a keyboard and monitor that are suitable for long periods of typing, editing and viewing business documents. Some monitors can be rotated and configured to allow documents to be viewed in portrait format. **Data security** is very important so a computer system in a business must be capable of storing data so that it is not lost accidently or through a faulty component (such as hard disk failure) or by being accessed by unauthorised users. Components must be chosen for their reliability to ensure that they have a long, useful life. The use of cheap components is not cost effective.

Configuring systems

Office computers have to be set up so that the office staff can perform their tasks.

A typical office computer will have a:

- suitable size monitor placed for easy viewing of documents with minimal eye or neck strain
- keyboard suitable for long periods of typing or entering data
- mouse for choosing options/selecting text
- large and fast hard disk to store and access company files
- DVD/CD-rewriter to load any new software and to make backups or archives of files
- network card for connecting to the company network to share files and for using the internet
- suitably placed case to hold the main components.

This computer will run a windows-based **operating system** such as Microsoft Windows, Apple OS or open-source alternatives such as Linux, and a range of office **applications** such as word processing, desktop publishing, spreadsheet and database software.

Microsoft and Apple operating systems are commonly used by businesses who pay for the use of the system and for technical support. The costs of the operating system, technical support and the applications that it will run can be quite high but the reliability and features offered make the cost worthwhile. Open-source operating systems are often free which saves businesses money as there is no need to purchase or licence the systems. However, open-source operating systems do not have the technical support that comes with software purchased from a large software developer so businesses using open-source software have to provide their own technical support and it can be expensive to employ technicians or software engineers. Businesses may find that purchasing or licensing software from major companies such as Microsoft or Apple is more cost effective in the long-term than employing their own highly skilled IT technicians to install and maintain open-source software.

An estate agent might also have presentation and image editing software, for example editing and using photos of properties in slideshows for its clients.

A leisure centre would also have specialised applications running on its laptops and smartphones that could be used by trainers and health centre staff to monitor the health and activities of its visitors.

Physical impairment

Users who are physically impaired can use a variety of devices to make their use of a computer easier:

Device	Use
Puff-suck switch	When the person blows or sucks, a switch is activated and can be used to select an item on screen or to send a command to the computer.
Braille keyboard	The keys have braille markings on them to allow people with visual impairment to feel the keys and choose one without seeing it.
Foot mouse	Feet, instead of hands and fingers, are used to press down on a foot mouse and to move the pointer on screen.

There are specialised software and settings that will allow physically impaired people to use computers:

Software or setting	Use
Text to speech software	Text is read aloud to visually impaired people who cannot see the screen properly. Sounds are made, or words are spoken, when commands are entered or carried out.
Speech to text software	Spoken commands are translated to actions that the computer carries out; spoken words appear as text in a document.
Zoom	Areas of the screen display are enlarged as a pointer is moved over the screen to enable text or images to be seen more easily.

Exam-type questions

1 Describe **one** hardware device that a visually impaired person would need to be able to type an email on her computer to send to an estate agent.   [2 marks]

2 Describe **one** special software application that a visually impaired person might use to compose an email on her computer to send to an estate agent.   [2 marks]

Remote working

People who are away from their usual place of work because they are travelling can gain access to their files over the internet. They can also send emails and transfer files while away from their office and access company files stored on company servers or in cloud storage.

This requires that the system that stores the files is configured to allow them to do so, can check that they have the proper authentication to be allowed to access the files, and can send and receive the files securely to make sure that no sensitive data is seen by others. The computer system being used must also be configured to access the remote storage.

Remote access can be by:

- sharing the desktop of a computer in the office, which means that the remote computer (a laptop, for example) appears to be using the desktop as if in the office
- using a virtual private network (VPN) which is a secure connection that appears to be part of the actual company network
- accessing files and folders using specialist software such as file transfer protocol (FTP) software.

However the access is carried out, a username and a password is required for the remote user. Also, the router that controls access to a company network has to be set up to allow remote access – if not, it will refuse access.

▶ Specification coverage

Factors that affect the
choice of system:
- Cost
- Availability
- User needs
- Data security

▶ What you will learn

How various factors affect
the choice of a computer
system.

How cost, availability, user needs and data security affect the choice of system

The correct choice of computing devices suitable for use by large organisations, small businesses and individuals is important because if the wrong, unsuitable or too expensive devices are chosen the organisation or business will not function efficiently and could go out of business.

The cost of purchase and maintenance of a computing device has to be considered. Receptionists and salespersons need computers that can carry out office tasks reliably but do not need expensive gaming machines or those that can perform complex video editing.

Desktop computers should have office and communication applications installed.

Desktop computers suitable for office tasks are readily available from suppliers who will build and supply them in sufficient quantities to keep the costs down.

Sales and other persons who travel and work away from the office must have a portable device such as a laptop or a smartphone that can carry out office tasks and communication with other staff and their employers. When choosing suitable portable devices, it is important to consider the features and cost of the device.

A very important consideration when choosing a portable device is the security of data that is stored on it. Users must set secure passwords that are needed to access the device and the files stored there. It is important to choose a device that makes it difficult for others to view data that is on the screen when working in public such as on a train or aircraft. Smaller screens, such as those on smartphones or tablets, are more difficult to read at a distance so others will find it more difficult to overlook the user.

Activity

1 Search the internet to help complete the following table to show the type of device and its suitability:

Portable device	Cost	Reasons why it is suitable for working while travelling	Reasons why it may not be suitable for working while travelling
Laptop with 15in screen			
Smartphone			

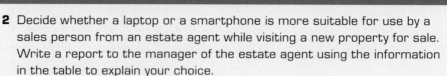

Activity

2 Decide whether a laptop or a smartphone is more suitable for use by a sales person from an estate agent while visiting a new property for sale. Write a report to the manager of the estate agent using the information in the table to explain your choice.

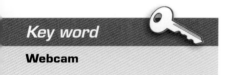

▶ *Specification coverage*

How peripherals can be connected to a computer device:
- Wired methods
- Wireless methods

▶ *What you will learn*

How cables (wired) and wireless methods are used to connect devices together.

Key word

Webcam

Connecting peripherals to a computer system

Computing devices can be connected together into a network so that data can be shared between the devices.

Computer peripherals

A computer peripheral is a device that is attached to but not actually part of the main computer system. Printers, scanners, microphones and **webcams** are examples of peripherals.

Peripherals can be connected by wires or cables and, more often now, wirelessly to a desktop or laptop computer and are then used directly from that computer.

The most common method of physically connecting a peripheral is to use a USB connection with a cable that plugs into a USB port on a computer.

Physical connections

USB

USB stands for 'universal serial bus' and is a standard way of connecting devices to each other. It allows fast data transmission that is suitable for transferring files such as documents and photographs between computers and printers, and from digital cameras to computers. USB has replaced older cable connection methods that were once used for printers and scanners.

FireWire

FireWire is a high-speed connection similar to USB and mainly used for connecting storage devices and transferring digital video. The hardware for FireWire is more expensive than that for USB so FireWire is not so popular.

Wireless connections

Wi-Fi

Many devices now use wireless connections to transfer data to printers and from cameras. Wireless connections (usually referred to as Wi-Fi) have the advantage that no physical cabling is needed, which means that connections are quick to make and data can easily be transferred. Wireless connections can be complicated to set up, slower to transfer data and may be less secure than cabled connections, but a wireless connection is more convenient for the user.

Wi-Fi connections can have a large bandwidth so that large amounts of data can be transferred quickly between devices.

Bluetooth®

Bluetooth® uses wireless technology to connect devices. It can be used to connect an input device such as a mouse but is more often used to exchange data (including photos) between mobile phones or to connect hands-free headsets to a mobile phone so that the phone can be used when driving or on the move.

Bluetooth® connections require devices to be 'paired' which means that each device has to use the same password key which helps keep data safe and secure from unauthorised users. It has a limited range and this also helps keep data secure.

Bluetooth® connections are low bandwidth so only small amounts of data can easily be transferred. Bluetooth® connections are often used to replace the wires that connect a mouse to a computer or headphones to a mobile phone because these connections do not need to transfer very large quantities of data very quickly.

Infrared connections

Wi-Fi and Bluetooth® connections do not need the devices to be in sight of each other but infrared connections do need the devices to be very close, usually within one metre. This can make an infrared connection very safe and secure and it is often used to transfer data between special business cards. Infrared connections can also transfer images very quickly.

Exam-type questions

1 Identify **one** wired method of connecting a printer to a laptop.   [1 mark]

2 Explain why a Wi-Fi and not a Bluetooth® connection would be used to connect a printer to a laptop.   [2 marks]

1

► *Specification coverage*

Connecting a computing device to an existing wireless network:
- Network names
- The use of security keys
- Appropriate firewall settings for public and private networks
- Remote working

► *What you will learn*

How computing devices can be connected together using wireless technology.

► *Key word*

Bandwidth

Connecting devices to wireless networks

Wireless connections

A wireless network uses radio waves to allow computing devices to connect together without the use of cables. This avoids the expense and time of laying network cables to each computer in a building. The connected devices can also be moved around if the user wants to work in a different place and as long as the device is within the range of the wireless network it will stay connected.

To be able to connect to a wireless network, the computing devices must have a wireless network card. This card is often referred to as having a Wi-Fi connection.

Portable devices can be connected to a wireless network quite easily as there is no need to attach a separate cable to each device. Laptops, tablet computers, smartphones and printers can easily be connected together or to a network using wireless connections.

Speed of data transmission

Wireless networks usually have slower rates of data transmission than wired networks and can appear to be slow to the user who has to wait longer for web pages to open, files to download or upload, or has jerky or stuttering playback of videos.

Bandwidth

The number of devices connected at one time and the **bandwidth** of the connection are the most important considerations when transferring large amounts of data over a wireless network connection. Watching a video over a Wi-Fi connection that several others are also using to play online games will be difficult if the connection does not have a high bandwidth.

Wireless connections can stop (or drop out) at the edge of the range or if obstacles such as walls are in the way.

Wi-Fi

Wi-Fi is a registered trademark of the Wi-Fi Alliance and is now often used as another name for a wireless network that connects to the internet. Public wireless networks (Wi-Fi 'hotspots') have been created so that portable devices can connect to the internet when away from the user's office or home. Wi-Fi hotspots can be found in cafes, hotels, libraries, and other public places, and have a range of about 20m indoors (and more outdoors) from the access point.

Service set identifier (SSID)

Each network has a unique name so that all the devices connected to it can identify it. The name of a wireless network is broadcast as the service set identifier (SSID). The SSID must be used by all the devices on that network if they are to be able to communicate with each other. SSIDs can be set manually by the person who administers the network or are set up automatically if the administrator leaves the name blank.

Public SSID

Network administrators can use a public SSID to broadcast to wireless devices in range of an access point. The automatic SSID broadcast can be disabled to improve network security and hiding the SSID can make it harder to detect the network but may give a false sense of security to the network manager because it does not prevent attacks on the network.

Security of wireless networks

Wireless networks can be less secure than wired networks because a wireless network is easier to connect to. There is no need for any cables and the radio waves are broadcast everywhere within range which means that potential unauthorised users are not easy to spot and that transmitted data can be intercepted by anyone. Security measures have to be used to prevent this happening.

Most wireless networks use encryption techniques so that the information is kept safe and secure from unauthorised users. The data is encrypted using an encryption key. This key is usually referred to as the 'password', the 'network key' or the 'security key' and to connect to, and transfer data over, an encrypted wireless network every device has to use the key.

WEP, WPA, WPA2, AES

WEP (wired equivalent privacy) was first used in 1999 to try to secure data transferred on wireless networks but this has been superseded by WPA, WPA2 (Wi-Fi protected access) and AES (advanced encryption standard), which are much more secure.

Exam-type questions

1 What are WPA and WEP used for? [2 marks]

2 Why is WPA preferred to WEP? [1 mark]

3 The SSID of a leisure centre's wireless network is 'LCentre'. How is this useful to people in the centre who wish to connect to the network? [2 marks]

Case studies

A leisure centre or estate agent might make use of a wireless network because the staff would be able to use their smartphones or laptops to connect to the centre's or estate agent's network and to access any shared files or data that they need. They would also be able to use the internet and to send and receive emails from anywhere in the centre or estate agent's offices.

To connect a laptop or smartphone to a wireless network:

- The member of staff would need to make sure that the wireless networking was switched on and ready to use. Wireless networking is not allowed in some areas or on board aircraft so all devices with wireless networking must have the facility to switch it off. Wireless networking also uses a lot of power so it is often switched off to conserve battery life in mobile devices.

- The first time it is used to connect, the laptop or smartphone will search for wireless networks and show their SSIDs so that the correct one can be chosen, the type of security used is chosen (such as WEP, WPA/WPA2) and the security key is entered so that the device is allowed to connect. The security key can be quite long but has to be entered accurately to ensure that the connection is allowed.

- The next time a connection is attempted the device will connect automatically.

The administrator of the network will set a unique SSID to identify the network and will also set a security key to try and make sure that only authorised devices and users can connect to the wireless network.

Remote access to networks

Staff can connect, using the internet, to the leisure centre or estate agent network when away from the centre or offices using a Wi-Fi hotspot if remote connections are allowed. This allows staff to update bookings and customer details, and use company facilities while away from the workplace on business. For example, an estate agent viewing a property for rent, or working from home.

Remote connections

Remote connections to company networks from the internet pose security dangers. If company networks are not kept secure then staff

and customer details such as addresses or financial details can be accessed by unauthorised users and used for fraud.

Company networks connect to the internet using a router which can be configured so that only authorised devices and users can access the internet. A **firewall** configured to prevent unauthorised access from the internet will help prevent access to data stored on the company network.

Firewall

A firewall can also be configured to allow authorised devices and users access from the internet so that staff can use company network facilities and data while away from the office.

Firewalls work by inspecting the network traffic as it arrives from the internet and, if it is not allowed, will stop it entering the company network. If the network traffic is allowed, the firewall will let the user access the network from outside. This can make the company network less secure, so a user ID and password must be set, and always asked for, when remote access is used.

User ID and password

Authorisation to use a network by **user ID** and **password** is usually carried out via a web page from the firewall or network that allows the user to enter the details before being allowed entry.

Staff working remotely will have their laptops or smartphones already configured to be recognised by the company network so they can access the network remotely.

Hotels that allow guests, or cafes that allow customers, to use their wireless networks provide the guest or customer with a user ID and password that is entered into a web page that appears automatically. Entering a correct user ID and password grants the user access to the wireless network and to the internet.

Exam-type questions

1 What is the purpose of a firewall between a company network and the internet? [1 mark]

2 How can a company set up its firewall to protect its network from unauthorised users? [2 marks]

3 Explain how a security key is used when setting up a connection to a network for the first time. [2 marks]

Specification coverage

How organisations can monitor employees:
- GPS location tracking
- Monitoring internet use and communications

What you will learn

How employees can be monitored by organisations.

How organisations can monitor employees

Introduction

Organisations might wish to know what their employees are doing and where they are during their working day. There are many reasons for this. The Police Force will want to know where its officers are so that they can be sent quickly to an incident. A bank will want to know where security staff delivering money to its branches are at all times so that the money is safe. A local council will want to know where its workers are if they are carrying out council duties because the council has a 'duty of care' to ensure that its employees are safe.

GPS tracking

The Global Positioning System (GPS) is a satellite-based system used by GPS receivers to find positions and times anywhere on the surface, or near to the surface, of the Earth. GPS uses four satellites for accurate position finding by the GPS device. The time and position information of each satellite is received by the device via signals from the satellites and used by the device to calculate its position on the surface of the Earth.

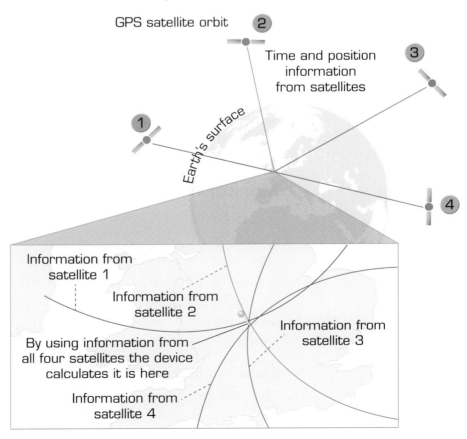

In-car GPS navigation system

GPS is accessible and free to anyone who has a receiver and can be used for navigation to or from anywhere that has a line-of-sight 'view' of four or more satellites.

GPS tracking uses the data from GPS satellites to find the precise location of the GPS tracking device. For example: if the device is attached to a car, the location of the car can be found; if it is held by a person, then that person can be found; or if the device is in a smartphone, then the phone can be located.

A GPS tracking device records its location at set intervals and this data can be transmitted using radio, a mobile phone connection or internet connection to a central computer. The location can be stored for later analysis or for display on a map so that the device can be 'tracked' in real time.

Uses of GPS tracking

Company vehicles or laptops can be tracked by fixing a GPS tracking device to them. People can only be tracked if they carry, and/or have attached to them, a GPS tracking device.

Some smartphones have GPS tracking built-in but most mobile phones, while they often have GPS receivers installed, do not have a tracking device. However, the location of a mobile phone can be traced to the nearest mobile phone access point – the place where it was last connected (but not necessarily used) to the mobile phone system.

Electronic tagging

The electronic tagging of criminals does not normally use GPS tracking but uses a device that is monitored by a base unit which will alert the authorities if the tag goes out of range. Tracking devices used to track criminals are similar to RFID tags in that they have to be monitored by receivers and do not actively send data about their location.

Monitoring internet use and communications

Companies have a responsibility to ensure that the use of the internet by their employees is for the purpose of doing their job and not for other, possibly inappropriate, use.

A member of staff in a leisure centre or an estate agent should only use the internet for work purposes and not for, for example, booking a personal holiday, online gambling or viewing pornography. Similarly, email use should not be for personal use but only for company business.

Email monitoring

Most companies allow their staff to use the internet or email for private use provided they do not abuse the privilege and bring the company into

disrepute. To ensure that staff do not abuse the privilege, most companies will block inappropriate websites from being used, scan emails to ensure that no viruses or inappropriate words are included, and keep automatic records and backups of all emails that are sent or received via the company systems. Some companies will record telephone conversations as well.

Company policy

Companies should have a policy about tracking employee internet use and telephone calls, and inform their employees that the company is monitoring their use of the internet and communications. The company must inform a caller to the company that the call may be recorded.

Exam-type questions

1 Describe **two** uses of GPS tracking in a smartphone. [4 marks]

2 Describe **two** other uses for GPS tracking. [4 marks]

3 Give **two** reasons why a leisure centre would want to monitor the use of the internet by its employees. [2 marks]

4 Why does a leisure centre inform its employees and callers that phone calls may be recorded? [1 mark]

Specification coverage

The different types of software:
- Operating systems
- Utility software
- Applications software:
  - Word processors and desktop publishing software
  - Spreadsheet and database management software
  - Multimedia software
  - Presentation and slideshow software
  - Photo-editing and graphics manipulation software
  - Video-editing software
  - Communications software
  - Gaming software
  - Web browsers
  - Apps for portable devices

Software

Operating systems and utility software are called system software.

Operating systems

Every computing device has an operating system. The purpose of the operating system is to manage the hardware and allow software to be run on the computer so that users can carry out tasks. Operating systems such as Microsoft Windows, Apple OS and iOS, and Android (developed by the Open Handset Alliance led by Google) use **graphical user interfaces** or **GUI**s. Linux is an open-source operating system that rivals Microsoft Windows and has similar office applications available for desktop and portable computers. Linux has been used as a basis for operating systems in mobile phones, televisions, TV set-top boxes, routers and video-game consoles.

A GUI uses windows to view the task or software in use, icons or small images to represent the task or choice, menus to provide choices for the user, and a pointer that can be moved around the screen by a mouse, or a touch screen operated using a stylus or fingers.

▶ **What you will learn**

The purpose and use of the different types of software.

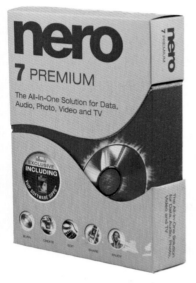

Nero utility software

Utility software

Utility software or utility tools add extra functions to an operating system, such as firewalls, backup software, managing printers and analysing computer performance. Many utilities carry out the more technical tasks that are needed to make a computing device work, such as managing disks by formatting, defragmenting and disk compression. Anti-virus software is another example of utility software.

Application software

Application software allows users to carry out useful tasks such as writing reports, surfing the web or using email.

Exam-type questions

1 Android and Linux are examples of open source software. Explain what is meant by 'open source software'. [2 marks]

2 What is the purpose of utility software? [1 mark]

Word processors and desktop publishing software

These applications are used for writing and producing documents on a personal computer. Both types of application allow the user to type words and add images to create letters, reports, books, magazines and newspapers without using commercial organisations to layout pages and print documents.

Desktop publishing software allows the user to have more control over the layout of pages and where items are placed on the page, but today most word-processing software has many features that were once only found in desktop publishing software.

Spreadsheet and database management software

Handling vast amounts of data, such as financial details and customer names and addresses, needs special software. Both spreadsheet and database management software are designed to handle numbers and text, and display graphics, so that they can be processed and displayed to provide information for the user.

Spreadsheets are designed to handle numbers and carry out calculations using functions and formulae. Spreadsheets can also create graphs to display the data or to show trends in the data. Spreadsheets have cells in which items of data such as values, labels, titles and formulae are stored.

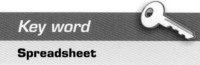

Key word

Spreadsheet

Key word

Database

Databases allow the entry, storage, editing, processing and retrieval of data. Companies store details such as their customers, clients, properties for sale or rent, or stock details. Databases can be used to store almost any type of data.

Databases are stored in files which are made up of records. A record is a collection of fields. A field holds one item of data. A database can be made of just one table of records – a flat file database – or it may hold many tables of records that are connected together by relationships – a relational database.

Databases can be used to store, search and sort data.

Multimedia software

Multimedia software allows different media sources such as text, images, audio, video and animations to be combined into a presentation for display to an audience.

Multimedia presentations can be linear just as in a movie or can contain navigation links that allow a user to choose their own route through the presentation.

Presentation and slideshow software

Presentation and slideshow software enable users to create a series of slides combining text and images. The slides can be shown individually or as part of a sequence. The slideshow can be displayed to an audience using a data projector and the speaker or presenter can move from one slide to another manually or by setting a timer in the software that changes the slides automatically.

The benefits of using presentation software are:

- the speaker can show text and images to illustrate a talk
- the slideshow can have links to other media or resources, for example a hyperlink to a web page or video
- the timings of the slide show can be made accurate and to suit the talk
- if manual changes between slides are used, the speaker can pause the show or change the order of slides to suit the audience
- if automatic slide changes are used, the speaker can talk without having to worry about the slides or the slideshow can be used without the speaker being present.

Photo-editing and graphics manipulation software

This software has a range of tools and features that are used to create or edit images. For example, photographs can:

- be edited to remove red eye or other unwanted blemishes (to enhance appearance) or cropped to remove unwanted parts of the image
- have elements cut off or out of the image
- be resized to fit frames in documents or for use in different devices
- have extra layers created to add new elements to the image.

Exam-type questions

1 Name **two** business documents that could be created using a word-processing application. [2 marks]

2 What would be the most suitable application for producing a short newsletter? Give reasons. [3 marks]

3 For each of the following tasks, state whether a spreadsheet or a database would be the most appropriate software application to use:

a) Calculating the total cost of a list of goods on an invoice. [1 mark]

b) Storing the details of all the members of a golf club. [1 mark]

c) Storing the details of properties for sale so they can be sorted into order of price. [1 mark]

d) Working out the weekly wages, with deductions for tax and insurance, of the staff of an estate agent. [1 mark]

Video-editing software

Video taken with a digital camera or captured from a webcam can be edited to remove unwanted sections, have sections joined together, and have effects (such as scene changes, titles or subtitles) added to make the video better for showing to an audience.

Communications software

Staff who want to have remote access to company networks and to exchange files, data and messages use communications software.

Suitable software includes file transfer applications, instant messaging clients, email clients, video and audio 'chat' applications.

Gaming software

Gaming software is used to create computer games for others to play. Most computer games for commercial sale are created by many programmers working on different parts of the game. The final game consists of the work from all the programmers combined together. These games are created on very powerful computers.

Simpler games can be created using freely available software for use on personal computers.

Web browsers

A web browser is used to display web pages from an intranet (a private company network) or from websites on the internet so that viewers can read text, view images, or play video or audio files.

Many web pages also include facilities for sending email and/or downloading files for later use or for viewing offline.

Apps for portable devices

Portable devices such as smartphones and tablet computers use 'apps', which are software applications written specially to make use of the limited memory resources, touchscreen and connectivity found in these devices.

Apps include those for navigation, accessing email, sending and receiving text messages, viewing web pages, storing photographs, purchasing goods, updating social network pages, and for many other tasks.

Configuring software

Operating systems, utility and applications software can be configured by the user to make them easier and more efficient in use.

Operating systems allow users to alter, for example, the language used by the system, the time and date, the resolution of the screen, the size and speed of movement of the mouse cursor, the size and colour of text on screen, as well as the arrangement of icons or windows on the screen. 'Sticky keys', audible warnings and enlarged sections of the screen ('zoom') can be set up to allow disabled users easier access to software.

Activity

Locate and use the accessibility options in an operating system to find out how the system can be altered to make it easier for disabled people to use the computer.

Exam-type questions

1 An estate agent has a multimedia presentation running on a large TV screen in its window. Describe **three** multimedia elements that it might include in the presentation. [6 marks]

2 Describe **two** ways a sales person for an estate agent might use a navigation app on a smartphone when showing a property for sale to a prospective buyer. [4 marks]

2

How to work with information and data to meet specific business needs

▶ Specification coverage

- Data capture methods:
  - ➤ Paper-based and online forms
  - ➤ Automated data capture systems
- How to design data capture forms to obtain specified information
- The factors that affect the choice of data capture methods:
  - ➤ Nature of the data to be captured
  - ➤ Cost and availability
  - ➤ Ease of use
  - ➤ Data security

▶ What you will learn

- How data is captured for use in computer systems.
- How data capture forms should be designed.

Key words

Data
Information
Data capture forms

Introduction

Data is 'raw' material that has not been processed and has no meaning. Information is data that has been processed to give it a meaning.

Collecting **data** and **information** for use in computer systems can be carried out automatically or manually. Automatic systems collect data with sensors such as temperature sensors or cameras; manual collection can be paper-based or online forms.

Information can be collected on forms, coded into data, and entered into a computer system that can process it and output it as information. For example, someone gives the information that their date of birth is 22 October 1950. This is coded and entered as 22101950 into a computer database, but when processed and output it is given as information in the form of 22-10-1950 or 22/10/50 or October 22nd 1950.

Data capture methods

Data capture forms

Data has to be collected in a suitable format so that it can be easily entered or input into a computer and then processed to provide the information required.

Data capture forms are pre-printed forms or online forms with prompts or questions and spaces for the answers.

Data can be collected manually by using paper-based (for example, questionnaires) or online forms. Online forms are used to enter data directly into computer systems, often over the internet using websites. This method of data capture is useful for collecting the details of new customers or prospective clients, for example by an estate agent or a leisure centre.

Some people do not like to have their details collected online so prefer to fill out paper-based forms themselves or have an employee do it for them.

Paper-based forms can be filled out by a member of staff who asks questions and then writes the answers on to the form. The questions and spaces on the form should be designed to make it easy for the questioner

Hints and tips

Make sure that you know the difference between data and information.

to ask the questions and get specific data from the customer or client ready to be transcribed into a computer system. Often the form will show examples of the way that data should be entered, and would be there to help a person who was filling out the form themselves.

PLEASE COMPLETE IN CAPITAL LETTERS ONLY

Mr ☐ Mrs ☐ Miss ☐ Ms ☐

First Name:

Surname:

Address:

Postcode:

D.O.B.:

Mobile:

Home Tel:

Email: _____

Employee Details

* Employee Id [ ]

* First Name [ ]

* Last Name [ ]

* Email [ ]

Phone number [ ]

Salary [ ]

Department [▾]

[Save]   * Required

Exam-type questions

1 For each of the following, choose whether it is better to use a paper-based form or an online form. Give a reason for your choice.

a) A questionnaire to hand out to visitors as they enter a leisure centre. [2 marks]

b) A form to be filled in by a receptionist to add a new member to the leisure centre. [2 marks]

c) A form to be used by an estate agent to collect the details of the interior of a house to rent while visiting the empty house. [2 marks]

d) A form to be used on a website for entering the details of houses for rent. [2 marks]

2 Why do some paper-based forms show examples of the data that has to be entered? [2 marks]

Unit 1 Understanding computer systems

Use the internet to find and examine at least five data capture forms and pick out the good points of each. Suggest ways that each form could be improved.

Designing data capture forms

When creating a data capture form, the number of spaces for an answer and the type of answer accepted will make sure that the data is collected in a suitable format.

Data such as temperature should be collected as numbers and names should be collected as text so that any character can be used.

People filling in paper-based forms can write whatever they wish on the form so it is important that the form has instructions or examples as guidance to make sure that the data collected is ready to be entered into a computer system.

The form below forces the person to space out the letters of the name properly and to tick boxes:

Address

Street	M A N O R	R O A D																	
Town	L O N D O N																		
County																				
Post code							

| Rented ☐ | Private ☑ | Local authority ☐ |

Online data capture forms can limit the type of data entered by using:

- **drop down menus**, the user is forced to choose from a pre-set selection of choices
- boxes to choose activities of interest
- a single-character text box for each letter of a name but this would be tedious for the user when entering a name so is not used often
- a pre-set format for a date so that all forms are completed in the same way
- **radio buttons** to force the person to make a single choice from several options
- validation rules to make sure that the data that is entered by the user is in the correct format and meets specific requirements (for example, a telephone number has the right number of characters and no spaces, or a postcode is in the right format) or to ensure specific questions have to be answered before the user can move to the next question so that all the data that is needed is actually collected.

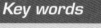

Key words

Drop down menus
Radio buttons

Data Collection Sheet

Please check that the information below Is correct.

Surname [   ]   Forename [   ]

Middle Name (s) [   ]

Gender [▾]   Date of birth [Day ▾] [Month ▾] [Year ▾]

Address [   ]

Post code [   ]

Please give details of all persons who have parental responsibility
and anyone else you wish to be contacted in an emergency.

Place them in the order you wish them to be contacted in an emergency.

Name	Relationship	Address	Contact number

Travel details   Please tick appropriate choice

Bicycle ○   Train ○   Bus ○   Walk ○   Car ○   Taxi ○   Other [   ]

There are some things to *avoid* when designing data capture forms:

- Using too small a font to be read easily.
- Making the boxes for writing or typing too small or not having enough of them or having too many boxes. For example, five boxes for the letters of a name is too few and 20 for a telephone number is far too many.
- Asking vague questions such as 'what do you like best?'
- Not specifying the format for data entry that you want. For example, a line on which to write a date of birth means that the format can be almost anything.
- Using overlapping choices to collect data. For example, about the number of times a person has used a website. The ranges should not be 0–5, 5–10, 10–15 because the ranges overlap.
- A single text box should not be used to collect an address as the data is not divided into first line, city and postcode which makes it very difficult to sort or search when stored on a computer system.

Activity

You have been given the task of creating a database of the cost, type and features of the latest smartphones sold online. Design a data capture form to collect data about smartphones, ready for entering into a database.

Exam-type questions

1 How can an online form be set up to make sure that the person using it enters only letters in their name? [3 marks]

2 How can a paper-based form be set up to make sure that the person using it enters only the correct number of characters in a postcode? [2 marks]

3 How can the owner of an online form make sure that all the important data is entered into the form? [4 marks]

Automated data capture systems

It is often necessary or convenient to capture data automatically, for example controlling a heating or air-conditioning system, when selling goods at a supermarket checkout or taking readings from a visitor during a workout in a leisure centre.

Sensors are used to collect data about physical parameters:

Sensor	Typical use
Temperature	Measuring the temperature of a room for use in a heating/air-conditioning system, a swimming pool for use in controlling the temperature of the pool, or the lava from a volcano.
pH	Measuring the pH level of a swimming pool for use in water quality control systems.
Light	Measuring the light level in a room for use in controlling lighting systems.
Pressure	Detecting the presence of a person standing on a door mat for use in opening a door automatically or setting off an alarm.

When collecting data for use in a computer system, various factors will affect how the data is captured.

Nature of information

The nature of the information to be collected has to be considered. Names, addresses and postcodes are made up of text (all sorts of characters including letters, digits and punctuation) but other data such as height or weight are made up of numbers. The type of data to be collected will determine the way it is collected.

Collecting the names and addresses of prospective customers by a supermarket for online shopping has to be done via an online form but taking the names of new members to a leisure centre can be done using a paper-based form that is filled in at the centre.

Location of information

The location of the information also determines how the data is collected. Data about environmental conditions in places which are dangerous to or unsuitable for humans, such as inside a nuclear reactor or the entrance to a volcano, in areas of extreme cold in the Arctic or Antarctic, or deep in the ocean are usually collected automatically by sensors. The use of sensors means that humans do not have to go to these places or, if they do go there, they do not have to stay there all the time.

The location does not have to be dangerous to use sensors. Often, it is more convenient to have the data collected automatically rather than have a human there all the time. Humans can be freed to do other jobs while the sensors automatically collect data. For example, the levels of water in a reservoir can be remotely monitored without a human visiting the reservoir each day.

Cost

The cost of collection of data is a consideration for some businesses. Small businesses will use paper-based forms because these are less expensive that the cost of the time and expertise for developing and using online forms and online payment methods.

Paper-based forms

Using paper-based forms to collect information from people can be costly. There are the costs of the paper and printing, the costs of the time taken by the person who uses the form to ask questions and then enter the data, the costs of transcribing the data from the form into the computer system and the cost of checking that the data has been entered accurately.

The data written on paper-based forms may not be easy to read if the hand-writing is not clear, may be incomplete, or may be wrong if the user does not answer with the truth. Online data capture forms are always clear to read as the answers are typed or coded in boxes, rules can be set up to make sure all the data is entered but there is nothing an online form can do to make a user answer truthfully.

Analogue and digital data

Analogue data is in continually varying form. Digital data is in the form of discrete values.

Data collected by sensors is in analogue form and has to be converted to digital form for use by computer systems. Sensors such as temperature, pH and light sensors are connected via an **analogue to digital converter** into a computer which can record the data for later use or display in reports or on screen. The data collected by these sensors could be used to control a heating system for offices, an air-conditioning unit for a shopping area, the temperature in refrigeration or freezer cabinets in a supermarket, or the temperature and water quality of a swimming pool.

Security of data

The data that is collected has to be kept secure. The personal details of customers, their credit card details and other information about them must be kept secure. This means preventing it from being accidently lost or damaged. For example, from being edited and altered so it is incomplete or no longer accurate, and preventing unauthorised users from accessing the data to copy or steal it for use in fraud or other activities such as advertising by sending unwanted emails to the customers.

Data can be kept secure with the proper use of backups, using passwords for access and by encrypting stored or transmitted data.

Exam-type questions

1 What is the purpose of a 'password'? [1 mark]

2 How could a leisure centre use the data collected from the sensors in its swimming pool? [4 marks]

Key words

Analogue to digital converter
Personal data

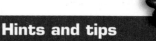

Hints and tips

You must know how **personal data** can be kept secure by businesses.

Case study: Supermarket

SaverShop is a large supermarket chain offering competitively priced branded products with lots of variety as well as their own less expensive brands. The SaverShop supermarket chain operates over 212 stores and employs in excess of 3000 staff.

The store is equipped with electronic point of sale (EPOS) system at its tills and these are linked to its stock control system. Staff working on the store floor use hand-held devices to check stock on the shelves and to keep in contact with other staff.

Office workers use desktop computers for their tasks and some managerial staff are supplied with laptops so they can move from store to store. All managers are supplied with a smartphone for use on store business.

Bar codes

All the goods in the stores have bar codes attached. The bar code contains data that can uniquely identify the item. When the bar code is scanned, the data is read and used to look up the details of the item in a database stored on the supermarket's computer system. The bar code is read by a bar code scanner/reader at the checkout.

The use of bar codes allows the use of self-service checkouts because all the information about the item is already on the store database and does not need to be entered again at the checkout.

Staff can also use hand-held or portable readers to scan the items on the shelves, count the number on the shelf, and send the data to the store computer system to update the database so the store knows how many items are in stock.

Matrix bar codes

Matrix bar codes, which have data coded in two dimensions, were first used in the motor car industry (they were invented for Toyota) and are often called QR codes – quick response codes.

The code consists of black modules arranged in a square pattern on a white background. This type of bar code can carry more data and can be read much faster than conventional bar codes

QR codes have in recent years become commonly used in advertising and packaging of consumer products, because they can be easily read by smartphones using a free app. Using QR codes that can be read by a smartphone allows the user to be given more information about the product very quickly, and can link directly to the manufacturer or retailer website to increase the chances of a sale.

RFID tags

Radio frequency identification (RFID) tags are small devices that use radio waves to transfer data from the tag to a computer system that can use the data to identify the item. RFID tags are used by supermarkets to automatically identify items, enable the tracking of items as they move around factories or warehouses, and can be attached to luggage at airports to enable the luggage to be tracked as it is moved to and from aircraft.

Near field communications

Near field communications (NFC) are used in smartphones to create radio links over a very short range, typically only a few centimetres or less. When using NFC, a smartphone is touched or waved very close to another device to exchange data such as a configuration for Wi-Fi or contactless financial transactions such as paying for parking. NFC sets itself up faster than Bluetooth® and there is no need for pairing but data transfer is slower than Bluetooth®.

NFC devices can be used to quickly pay for goods or services by waving a phone containing an NFC device close to a receiver. Fast data transfer of transaction details similar to those in credit cards allows 'mobile payment'. Google Wallet is such a system where users store their credit card information in a virtual wallet and use an NFC device at terminals that accept credit cards. The payment is contactless and can be quick.

Case study: RFID tags

RFID tags are fixed to clothing, DVD cases and expensive bottles of alcohol such as spirits, wines and champagne.

The tags have to be removed by a special device before the item leaves the store. Checkout operators remove the RFID tags from the items as they are sold.

If the RFID tag is not removed, a sensor at the door of the store will detect the RFID tag, a computer system attached to the sensor will be alerted and set off an alarm to attract the attention of security staff.

The advantages of using RFID tags instead of bar codes for security are that RFID tags are small so are easily attached to items, can be read at a distance very quickly and are not easily damaged or removed by shoppers. While the receiving equipment is more expensive than a bar code reader, RFID tags are quite cheap to use and install on goods. Also, RFID tags can be read automatically and at a greater distance than bar codes, which makes them useful for security. An item being removed from a store with an RFID tag still attached will be detected at a distance by an RFID scanner without the person knowing and the system can set off an alarm.

Hints and tips

You must make sure that you know how and why retail stores make use of both bar codes and RFID tags.

Exam-type questions

1 Give **two** reasons why RFID tags instead of bar codes are used to tag goods. [2 marks]

2 Why are QR codes useful for people who have smartphones? [3 marks]

3 What information is stored in a bar code? [2 marks]

4 Give **two** uses, other than tagging goods in a supermarket, for RFID tags. [2 marks]

▶ **Specification coverage**

- How to code information for use in a spreadsheet or database
- Data verification and validation methods
- File formats for storing data:
  - ➤ Proprietary formats
  - ➤ Open formats

▶ **What you will learn**

How data is stored and used in spreadsheets or databases.

Data

Before entering data into a spreadsheet or database, consideration should be made on how it is to be stored and used.

Text can be used to store any type of data. It can be sorted and searched but calculations cannot be carried out on data stored as text.

If calculations are required, for example adding up totals, number of items sold or in stock, the data has to be stored as a number. Using numbers also allows data to be sorted into numerical order. Currency and dates are also stored as numbers so that calculations can be made. For example, the total cost of items being bought at a checkout or how long a sales period lasts.

Data types

The different types of data are shown in the following table:

Data type	Description	Example of data	Typical use
Text	Any character	Abc|<.<;;65 3	Names of items or people. Telephone 'numbers' are stored as text because telephone numbers can have spaces and leading zeros.
Integer number	Whole numbers	19243	Number of items in stock, number of people in a shop, number of tickets to a cinema performance sold in one day.
Real number	Any number, with or without decimal places	12.99	Prices, height, weight
Date	Time	20/07/12	A date, e.g. 20 July 2012
Boolean	True or False	There are only two choices: 1 or 0, yes or no, M or F	Storing the gender of a person.
Image	A graphic file	A photograph	A photograph of a member of a club shown on a membership card.

It is important to code data properly or else it will not be able to be used to display the information that the user wants from the spreadsheet or database. For example, storing the number or items in stock as text will not allow the total to be calculated so a supermarket manager will not know how many items there are for sale or have been sold.

Coding data

To save space in a spreadsheet or database file, data can be coded.

Examples of coding of data include:

- Y or N instead of Yes or No
- M or F instead of male or female
- Mr instead of Mister
- Mrs instead of Mistress
- 120930 instead of 12 September 1930

To make it easy to locate the details of items in a stock database, each item is given a code that can be searched for or sorted into order. It is quicker for the computer system to do this with codes than with complicated names. For example, item '98076' is used instead of 'blue, large, breadbin with a lid'.

Exam-type questions

1 For each of these examples of data, choose a suitable data type for storing it in a database:

   a) 26 March 1969 [1 mark]

   b) CB21 7WX [1 mark]

   c) Boy or Girl [1 mark]

   d) Your own name [1 mark]

   e) 456 [1 mark]

2 Why would Male or Female be entered by a receptionist as M or F into a database? [1 mark]

Making sure that data is accurate

Any data that is stored in a spreadsheet or database and used to retrieve useful information must be accurate. Accuracy of data is vital to all organisations.

There are two methods of ensuring data is accurate: verification and validation. Neither method makes sure that the data is correct – only that it is entered accurately and is the right sort of data.

Verification

Verification checks that data is entered exactly as it is shown on the original data capture sheet. This ensures that the original answers to questions are entered into the spreadsheet or database.

A visual check to see if the data in the computer system is the same as that on the original questionnaire is often all that needed, but is only suitable if there is not too much data to check.

For large amounts of data, the data is entered twice by different operators, and the computer system checks one set of data against the other. If any differences are found, the computer system will report the differences to the operators. For example, entering the details of hours worked by employees ready for working out their weekly wages.

Sometimes new data has to be entered very accurately the first time so double entry is used. For example, when entering a new password into an online form, the password is requested twice so that the two entries can be checked against each other and any differences will cause an error message to be displayed. The user will have to try inputting the password entry again until a match is made.

Validation

Validation checks data as it is entered into a spreadsheet or database to make sure it is allowed into the system. As the operator types in the data, the system checks it against the validation rules and if it is not allowed an error message is shown. If it is allowed, the data will be stored.

Validation uses rules to make sure that data is reasonable and abides by the rules set up when the spreadsheet or database was made.

Validation checks include:

- Presence check – makes sure that data is actually entered by the user. This would be used to make sure that all the important details are entered into an online form for a new membership or account.
- Data type check – makes sure that data is the correct type. For example, a credit card number is made up of only numbers, a person's name does not have numbers at all.

Student_ID	Student_Name	Latest_Test_Result
0001	Ashley	72
0002	Mo	88
0003	Anand	65
0004	Claire	91
0005	Jaz	88
0006	Stephen	77
0007	Tomasz	76
0008	Ruta	89

Search

Student_ID	0010
Student_Name	Ben
Latest_Test_Result	75

Add

Enter Student_ID 0009 First

OK

About
Help

- Format or picture check – makes sure that the data is in the correct format. For example, DD/MM/YYYY (day, month, full year) for a date such as 22/10/1950.
- Range check – makes sure that the data is within set limits. This would be used to check that a person's date of birth is such that the person is, for example, at least 18 years of age and less than 55 years of age, which could be the age range allowed for the use of certain facilities at a leisure centre, for example.
- Character check – makes sure that only allowed characters can be entered and others are rejected. For example, a postcode does not have # or @ or punctuation marks.

There are other checks that can be made on data. For example, a check digit is added to a number calculated from a collection of digits. When the digits are read from a bar code, for example, the check digit is calculated again to make sure that they have been read accurately.

Exam-type questions

1 Why should the prices of using the facilities in a leisure centre not be stored as text? [1 mark]

2 Explain how a salesperson in an estate agent could make sure that the data he/she collected on a data capture form of details of a house for sale were accurately shown on the business website? [3 marks]

3 A leisure centre employs a large number of people who work different hours for different rates of pay. All the details of their hours worked and pay rates have to be entered into the computer system each week to make sure that they are paid the correct amount. How can the data be verified to make sure it is correctly entered? [4 marks]

4 What is a check digit? [3 marks]

File formats

Files created by software applications are stored on storage media so that they can be retrieved for use later.

Each software application stores its files in a way that it can use efficiently. Different applications use different **file formats** to store their data and this helps when opening a file. A particular file format will tell the operating system which application needs to open it.

Some operating systems use extensions to the file name to show the file format while some look inside the file to find out.

Key word

File formats

Proprietary formats

Proprietary formats are those owned by commercial companies and are only used by the software made by the owners. Open formats are those formats that the owners allow others to use.

Microsoft uses extensions and some of the most common proprietary formats are shown in the following table:

Format's file extensions	Meaning	Typically used to store
.doc .docx	Microsoft Word document	Word-processed letters and other typed documents
.xls .xlsx	Microsoft Excel document	Spreadsheets
.ppt .pptx	Microsoft PowerPoint slides	Slideshow presentations
.fla	Adobe Flash movie/animations	Animations/movies
.wma	Windows media audio	Audio/sounds

Open formats

Open formats are used by a variety of software applications and can be used to transfer data between applications.

Some open file formats are shown in the following table:

Format's file extensions	Meaning	Typically used to store
.aac	Advanced audio coding	Audio/sounds stored without loss of data, used by a number of manufacturers
.rtf	Rich text format	Word-processed documents
.csv	Comma separated values	Lists of data and often used when transferring data between software packages
.exe	Executable file	Applications that can be run on computer systems
.txt	Text	Unformatted text files
.pdf	Portable document format	Formatted documents
.mp3	MPEG audio layer 3	Audio/sounds stored with loss of data when the files are compressed
.aiff	Apple's audio format	Audio/sounds
.wav	Microsoft's audio format used by many computer systems	Audio/sounds

The file format used will depend on the software being used at the time and what the user wants to do with the file.

Exam-type questions

1 Why do applications save files with a file extension? [1 mark]

2 Explain what is meant by a proprietary file format and an open
source format? [2 marks]

3 Identify **two** file formats that could be used to store notes made
by an estate agent as he/she interviews people who might want to
rent a house. [2 marks]

Choosing an appropriate file format

The choice of file format to use depends on:

- what the file contains and how best to store it
- which software application has created the file
- what the user intends to use the file for.

While all data stored on computer systems is in a digital format, how
the content of the file is arranged is different depending on the data
being stored. The contents of a file may be video, audio, images, text
or numbers but all have to be stored in a way that ensures that the data
can be retrieved and used again at a later date whenever needed.

A DTP file saved on a computer disk will contain text, numbers
and images and all these have to be linked so that when the file is
opened again, they all appear in the correct place. For example, a DTP
application will save its files using the most suitable format to do this.
Microsoft Publisher uses its own file format but you can use any of the
following formats to save files:

Activity

Load your favourite image/ graphic manipulation software and create a simple image, then choose 'save as'. Look at all the file formats that can be used to save the image and find out why you might choose:

- jpeg
- png
- TIFF
- GIF

to save your file.

A person creating a file using Microsoft Publisher would normally choose to save it as a 'Publisher' file but may choose one of the others, for example:

- PDF which can be opened by free PDF readers on most computers and mobile devices such as smartphones with no need to have Microsoft Publisher installed.
- Plain Text – only the text is stored properly but this is useful for extracting the text from the document.
- Rich Text Format which is useful for transferring the document to other computing devices and applications.
- Web Page formats which are used when the document is going to be used on a website.
- PostScript format which is used for printing purposes.

Choosing a file format for saving an image is important as most image file formats compress the image and may lose some of the details.

Files that are intended to be shared should be saved in a format that most, if not all, computers and portable devices can use. Also, sharing files over the internet will influence the choice of format because very large files can take a very long time to send or receive.

Activity

Complete this table by stating the advantages and disadvantages of using each of the formats shown to store a word-processed document which has three pages, each with several text paragraphs and a few images.

File format	Advantages	Disadvantages
Rich Text Format		
PDF		
Plain Text		
HTML		

Exam-type question

1 Audio files are often stored using the MP3 format for use on portable devices. Why is this? [2 marks]

Specification coverage

Security measures used
when storing data:
- Computer security:
  - Usernames/passwords
  - Access rights/
    permissions
- Document security:
  - Passwords
  - Restricting access to or
    editing of content
  - Data encryption
- Physical security

What you will learn

How data can be stored
safely and securely.

Security measures used when storing data

Data must be kept safe and secure when being stored or transmitted by computing devices.

Data can be kept safe from loss or accidental damage (being changed or corrupted) by careful use of the computing device.

Users can try to keep their own data safe by:
- saving their work regularly
- making regular backups and never saving only one copy of their work
- shutting down the computer properly
- storing storage media such as CDs and other removable media carefully to avoid loss or damage.

Backups and secure storage methods are used by many organisations to safeguard their data.

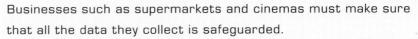

Case studies

Businesses such as supermarkets and cinemas must make sure that all the data they collect is safeguarded.

When a member of staff such as a manager or check-out operator wants to use the supermarket computers and network, a user ID and password must be entered.

A user ID will identify the user to the system so the user profile or settings are loaded ready for the member of staff to use. A user ID is the 'user identity' or username.

A password is required for security purposes. The password will make sure that the person logging into the system is the person that should be using that user ID because only that person will know the password. For this reason, passwords must be kept private and told to no one else, changed regularly and not written down. Passwords should also be made up of at least six characters, a mixture of upper and lower case letters and numbers, and with some spaces.

Passwords should also be easy to remember but not easy to guess.

A supermarket will assign usernames to its staff but the staff will have to set their own passwords and change them regularly. Many organisations may force their staff to change their passwords at intervals and may not allow them to use passwords that they have previously used.

Exam-type questions

1 What is the reason for having a username (user ID) when logging into a computer system?   [1 mark]

2 Give **four** 'rules' that should be followed when creating passwords.   [4 marks]

Access rights and permissions

All files and folders have **access rights** and **permissions** that can be adjusted to control who can read, edit, alter or save the file.

Organisations use access rights and permissions to control which files employees are allowed to look at by setting different access permissions to the folders or files. Managers would have access to folders of files that other office staff would not – a personnel manager would be able to look into the files and folders that contain staff personal details but a warehouse manager would not have the access rights and permissions to do this.

Files and folders can be protected by setting the access rights to read-only so that they cannot be altered.

Individual documents can be password protected so that only authorised staff can open the file to read and edit the contents.

As well as protecting the whole document with a password, restrictions can be set on certain parts of the document. This is useful in spreadsheets, for example, where formulae must not be changed when an office worker is entering data about prices. The data on prices can be changed but the calculations using the formulae must remain the same.

Physical security

Supermarkets use security guards to protect the physical goods in their stores. At the same time, guards can be posted at the doors of offices where the computers are used or at the doors of the rooms where the data is stored on the computer servers.

As well as locking the doors and only giving keys to the staff that are allowed to enter the area, electronic security locks that need a code or RFID tags in staff badges to open can be used to keep out unauthorised people.

Security badges

Badges with RFID tags can be used to control where staff are allowed to go – some staff will have access to different areas than others. If a staff member has their job role changed, all that is necessary is to alter the data on the RFID tag to change the areas into which the person can go.

Other physical security includes not having the computer systems on the ground floor with windows that can be broken to gain access, having bars or strengthened glass on windows and doors, and having strong doors.

A simple way to stop people seeing what is on a computer screen is to face it away from windows, doors and walkways.

Exam-type questions

1 Describe **three** ways that a salesperson in a small business, such as an estate agent, can make sure that data about a new customer is kept secure while it is being entered. [4 marks]

2 A staff member in a leisure centre has a badge that she is required to wear all the time she is working at the centre. Why? [4 marks]

Encryption

However difficult access to computer files is made by using passwords and other methods of keeping out unauthorised users, data may still be copied or stolen. Encryption will help to prevent the data being used by unauthorised people.

Data can be scrambled using **data encryption software** when it is stored or transmitted between computers over networks.

Data encryption software uses an **encryption code** or **key** to scramble (encrypt) the contents of data files. The proper code is needed to unscramble the file (decrypt it) so it can be read and used. If the encrypted file is accessed by anyone without the proper code to unscramble it, the data is meaningless.

Digital signatures are an example of encryption and are used to check that a website or a message is authentic.

Using an encryption key to encrypt and decrypt a message

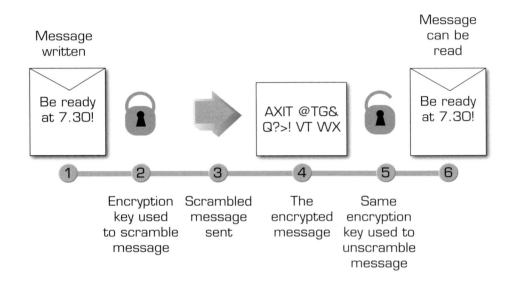

The data held by businesses about their customers and their financial details are encrypted when stored on disks so that if anyone steals the data the details cannot be used.

When customers buy goods online, book cinema tickets online or enter personal details into any website, the data should be encrypted before being transmitted. This will keep the details from being read or used by others even if they are intercepted. Everyone should check that the website they are using to enter personal detail uses encryption.

A secure website using encryption will use **https** instead of **http** in the URL and will show a small padlock.

Different web browsers indicate the use of https in different ways.

Exam-type questions

1 What is meant by an encryption key? [1 mark]

2 What is the reason for encrypting data in a backup? [2 marks]

Key words

https
http

Activity

Try out different web browsers and find out how each shows the use of https for secure sites.

Specification coverage

Data transferring technologies:
- Wired and wireless methods
- Mobile data transmission
- Methods of exchanging data

What you will learn

- How data is exchanged safely and securely.
- Factors affecting choice of method of transfer.

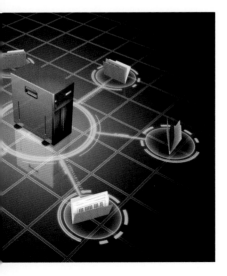

Data transferring technologies

Data can be transferred between computing devices by networking the devices together. Homes, schools and companies can have their own computer networks using the devices listed in Chapter 1.

Internet

The internet is a very large, global network to which other networks can be connected and which can be used to transfer data between networks. The internet uses public telecommunications and is available for almost everyone to use. This means that any data transferred over the internet is not very secure so important data must be encrypted first.

Connecting networks

Networks can be connected using cables (wires) or by using wireless technologies.

Wired networks connect each device together with a cable. In wired networks, there is usually a hub, switch or router to which all the devices such as desktop computers, servers and printers connect. In home networks, the router that connects to the internet will have sockets for connecting wired devices. Wired networks can work at very high speeds.

Wired networks can be expensive to set up as the costs of installation and cables can be high for larger networks. Also, the cables can be difficult to place in older buildings and may be unsightly in homes.

Wireless networks use radio waves to connect devices. There is a wireless access point to which all the devices connect.

Wireless networks are often easy to set up but can be complicated to configure and make secure. Portable devices such as smartphones and laptops have wireless network cards built in and can easily connect to a wireless network. As there are no wires, the devices can be moved around and used anywhere in range of a wireless access point but the speed is usually slower than for wired networks.

Connecting while mobile or travelling

Many hotels, cafes and shops offer free wireless networking to their guests and customers but some charge for its use. Some of the charges can be very high.

Mobile phones, smartphones and other portable devices can also use the mobile phone telecommunications networks to connect to networks and the internet. These mobile communication networks, called 3G or 4G networks, which means third generation or fourth generation, offer much slower speeds than wired or wireless networks but can be used for voice calls, mobile internet access, video calls and mobile TV access. 4G networks have a greater bandwidth, offering faster downloading and uploading of files than 3G.

Networks are used to transfer data between computing devices. Most networks use a server to store and allow access to data by users. Home networks may have a media server that can stream videos or audio to devices such as laptops or smartphones. Video and audio can be streamed from PCs without the need for a dedicated server but the PC has to be on all the time to do this.

Emails

Emails are sent from a desktop or portable device to an email server which sends the emails to other servers and then to the email inbox of the recipient. Using portable devices and wireless technology or mobile communication networks allows a person to send and receive emails from anywhere that has an access point. People can keep in touch with others while travelling for business or on holiday.

Email was originally designed for sending simple messages but it is now possible to attach files such as photographs, documents and video for sharing with others.

File sharing

Files can also be shared using a server. The file is uploaded to the server where it is stored until another person accesses and opens it.

Key word

Peer-to-peer

Peer-to-peer file sharing is used to transfer a file directly from a device to another without using a server. Peer-to-peer file sharing is useful when sharing photographs between mobile phones using Bluetooth® as it is quick and simple to do. Peer-to-peer file sharing, however, is often used to share illegally copied software or files because it does not use a server and is not easily discovered.

Cloud computing

Many companies now offer file storage facilities on their own servers that can be accessed by others over the internet. This is known as 'cloud' computing or storage because the users often do not know exactly where the servers are based and only access their files on the servers over the internet. The company hosting the servers is responsible for ensuring that the data is kept safe and secure. This type of storage, although expensive for large capacities, can be cost effective for smaller businesses that do not have to have their own servers or employ IT technicians to maintain them.

Factors affecting the choice of method of transfer

When choosing a method of transferring data between computers, the size of file, the type of data in the file, the location of the data, the destination of the data and how quickly the user wants the data to arrive are amongst the factors that should be considered.

Cost is not a major consideration, unless using postal services or couriers with guaranteed or insured delivery, but even the use of writable CDs or DVDs, USB memory sticks or email incurs some cost.

Transferring small files between two computers that can be physically visited, for example computers on the same desk, in the same room or building can be done using USB memory devices. The file is copied onto the device, the device taken to the other computer and the file copied or moved from it. This method of transfer can be quite quick if the two computers are not far apart. It is also a secure way of transferring data because, unless the USB memory stick is lost or stolen, the data is difficult to intercept.

Writable CDs or DVDs can also be used but writing the data to a CD or DVD can take a long time.

Small files can easily be sent by email as **attachments** and emails usually arrive anywhere in the world quite quickly. However, email requires the recipient to login and collect the email so delivery depends on when the email is collected or received in an inbox.

Transferring files over networks, both wired and wireless, is a convenient way of transferring files of all sizes although very large files can still take some time. Video and audio files are often large and these will take a long time to transfer as will large graphic files.

File transfer is usually faster over wired networks than wireless because of their larger bandwidth, but wireless networks can be more convenient to connect to, especially when away from the home or office. The security of data being transferred must be considered when using wireless networks.

Security is a major consideration when transferring data. Carrying data on CDs, DVDs or USB memory sticks when travelling or sending them though ordinary mail risks losing them, being intercepted by unauthorised people and the data stolen or misused. Encrypting data can help make it more secure.

Sending data by email is not secure and confidential documents should not be sent by email or, if they have to be sent by email, they should be encrypted.

USB memory device

Writable CD and DVD

Key word

Attachment

Exam-type questions

1 Explain **two** advantages of using wireless networking instead of
  wired connections in a store.   [4 marks]

2 Explain **two** disadvantages of using wireless networks in a store.   [4 marks]

Case study: Supermarket

Supermarkets use wired networks to which desktop computers
and checkout tills are connected. However, some department stores
are using wireless connections to their checkouts so that they can
easily alter the store arrangements or move the checkouts without
having to rewire buildings.

A large supermarket will give its staff wireless devices for checking
stock levels on shelves and for communicating with each other.
Staff can move around the store reading the bar codes of items on
shelves and entering the number of items on the shelf. The data will
be sent wirelessly back to the central stock computer to keep stock
information up to date. Used with the data from the checkouts, the
supermarket can make sure that new stock is ordered and delivered
before it has sold all the items it has in stock.

Data transfer speeds

Wired networks are usually faster than wireless networks. In practical
terms, this means that more data can be transferred in a set time over
wired networks than wireless networks. Bandwidth is usually measured
in bits per second. High-speed networks will have bandwidths of
megabits per second – millions of bits per second.

Bandwidth

The available bandwidth will determine how fast a file such as a video
or audio file can be downloaded. Higher bandwidths will allow video to
be played – or streamed – over the internet without being downloaded
first. Digitally compressed video and audio files can be played on
smartphones provided the device has a connection to the internet with
a high enough bandwidth. 3G mobile connections are just about good
enough but 4G mobile connections are much better for playing streamed
video because of the greater bandwidth available with 4G connections.

File compression

Compressing digital video and audio files to make them small enough to be streamed over low bandwidth connections allows them to be played on mobile phones, smartphones and other devices while the user is mobile. However, highly-compressed video and audio is poor quality and only suitable for small devices.

Exam-type questions

1 Why are video and audio files compressed? [2 marks]

2 Why is using a high bandwidth connection important when trying to view video being streamed from the internet? [2 marks]

► Specification coverage

Use of backup and recovery systems:
- Data storage media
- Backup frequency
- Automated versus manual systems
- Archiving

► What you will learn

- How backups can be created and used for recovery.
- The difference between backups and archives.

Key words

Backup
Archive

Tape drive

Backups and recovery

Backups are copies of data or files that are currently in use. Backups are made regularly and stored away from the computer system, preferably in another building in a secure place.

Archives are copies of data or files that are no longer needed for day-to-day use. Archives are made at less frequent intervals than backups and are stored away from the computer system. Archived data is not used often but is useful for reference purposes.

Backups in organisations

Creating backups

A supermarket will make backup copies of its data and files every day, usually at a set time, after most of the day's work has been done. Banks and other financial institutions make backups every few minutes because their data is so important.

Organisations such as supermarkets have huge amounts of data so writable CDs or DVDs or USB memory sticks do not have enough capacity. Tape drives and extra hard disks are therefore used to store the backups and archives of large companies. The tapes used in backup tape systems have a large capacity but are expensive. Extra hard disks also have very large capacities but are not so expensive.

Backups created by organisations are kept safely so that they are protected from theft or fire. The data on the backups is often encrypted so that even if the backups are lost or stolen, no one without the encryption key will be able to understand the data.

Unit 1 Understanding computer systems

Creating backups is so important that most large organisations will be prepared to spend large sums of money to ensure that they have adequate backups that can be used to recover any lost data.

The expense of using their own tape drives or additional hard disks can be too much for smaller businesses so many use 'cloud storage' or online backup services. With these, the backups are stored on servers managed by external companies who charge for the service but take responsibility for providing the systems and security for the data being backed up. The cost of these services can be much lower than paying for in-house IT technicians to manage and run backup systems.

How cloud storage can be used by small businesses for backups

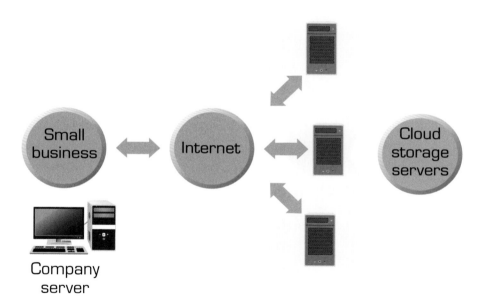

Activity

Find out what is meant by the 'Grandfather, Father, Son' method of creating backups using removable media.

Backup frequency

In many organisations, a backup will be created automatically at the end of each working day after business has been concluded. This is often done during the night when employees are not using the system.

Some organisations such as banks or large supermarkets will make backups much more often. Banks make backups every few minutes so that the latest transactions are safe and secure. Smaller businesses do not need to make backups as often as banks but should do so each day.

Creating backups at home

Home users should also make backups at regular intervals to make sure that they do not lose valuable documents, photographs and other important data.

Backups of data from home computers are made onto removable media such as writable CDs or DVDs. USB flash memory sticks can also be used. These removable media only have a relatively small capacity so are only suitable for making backups of a small amount of data.

Using **removable media** for backups means that the media can be stored safely and securely away from the computer systems, usually in a different building in a locked area. Backups of data must also be kept secure. Data and files kept for backup purposes should be encrypted.

Using removable media for archives has the same benefit as when using removable media for backups: it can be stored safely and securely away from the computer system. Archives should also be encrypted.

Using writable CDs or DVDs or USB memory sticks for frequent backups is easy but can also be costly as so many will be needed. Eventually there will be piles of CDs or DVDs that could present a storage problem. These forms of media are also easily lost.

As well as keeping backups of important data or files, backups of whole computer disks or systems can be made. An 'image' of a computer disk can be made. This takes a snapshot of the whole disk including the operating system and can be used to recreate the whole disk contents.

A removable hard disk is also suitable for making backups at home because it can hold a large amount of data such as that needed to store a backup of a whole system.

Exam-type question

1 Complete the following table by choosing a suitable backup medium and giving a reason for each of the backup tasks shown. [6 marks]

Backup task	Choice of backup medium	Reason(s)
Backing up a complete server in a bank		
Backing up a laptop's files in a small business		
Backing up a collection of photographs from a smartphone while travelling		
Backing up a folder of small documents from a laptop		

Backup frequency

Home users do not need to make backups every day but should make backups of important files every so often to make sure that data can be recovered if it is lost. In schools, it is important to make backups of schoolwork in case it gets deleted or corrupted in use. People should be advised not to work on the original copy of any file in case it is corrupted in use or some of it is accidently deleted.

Recovering data or files using a backup

If a collection of data or a file is lost, damaged or altered by accident, a backup can be used to restore the original file by copying the backup data or file back into its original place.

A **disk image** can be used to restore a whole hard disk.

A backup will restore the data, file or disk to the condition it was in when the backup was made. For this reason, backups must be taken at frequent and regular intervals or else the most recent work will be lost.

Incremental backups can be used to restore the latest data and files quite quickly.

Many backup systems allow individual files to be accessed and restored without the need for a full restoration of the whole system. Allowing individual files to be restored is much quicker and more convenient for the user. In the home, the ability to restore individual files that have been lost or deleted is the reason why most people keep backups.

Archives

Archives are collections of data that are needed but no longer in everyday use.

Archives can be made in the same way as backups – copies of the whole disk or of individual files can be made – and the original data or files are then removed from the computer system and stored elsewhere. With backups, the original data is not removed because it is still needed for everyday use.

Archives are, for example, used to store data about sales for the previous financial year, records of students who have left school, details of previous customers or suppliers who no longer have dealings with the business, or of employees who have left. The data has to be kept so that it can be used for reference in case the information is needed, for example, for tax purposes or to contact an ex-employee or ex-student.

Key word

Disk image

Activity

A small corner shop sells newspapers and magazines, groceries and drinks. It uses a desktop computer system in its back office for managing its finances and keeping track of its stock.

Write a report for the owner to explain how they should make and keep backups of their files. Also, explain why it should archive its records from previous years.

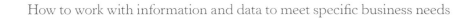

Factors affecting the choice of method of backup or archive

Type of method used for backup	Cost	Ease of use	Data security
Tape system	Expensive device and media	• Tape needs replacing after every backup • Tapes are very susceptible to damage	• Data is encrypted • Tapes must be stored securely as they are quite small in size and easily stolen or lost
Additional hard disks in a dedicated server	A separate server can be expensive to set up	• Requires data to be transferred to separate server so can be complex to set up and schedule • Used by large organisations	• Data is transferred over network to another computer system so is encrypted • Disks are fixed in the systems that are stored securely so not easily stolen
External hard disks	These can be relatively cheap to use	• Connection is often via a USB connection, which is not always present on devices and data transfers can be slow compared to dedicated hard disks	• The disks can be easily damaged by movement and can be lost or stolen • Data can be encrypted
Writable CDs and DVDs	Media is cheaper than hard disk but may work out more expensive if large quantities are needed	• A new CD or DVD has to be placed in the drive each time because capacity is not enough for large organisations to create full backups • Very suitable for home use. For example, making backups of photos or documents	• Media can be easily stolen or lost if not securely stored • Most people do not encrypt their photos or files when using DVDs or CDs to make backups
USB memory sticks	Cheap to buy	• Will work in almost all computer systems, although not suitable for most smartphones and many tablet computers which do not have USB connections for external memory sticks	• Most USB memory sticks have the facility to encrypt the data stored on them • A password is needed to access the data on the stick

Exam-type questions

1 Explain why organisations keep archives of their computer files.   [2 marks]

2 Explain why a bank creates backups of transactions every few minutes but a small shop creates a backup only once a day.   [4 marks]

3

How ICT can be used to support business working practices

▶ *Specification coverage*

Communication methods such as:

- Voice telephones
- SMS
- Instant messaging
- Email
- Chat rooms
- Forums
- Bulletin boards
- Voice over internet protocol (VoIP)
- Videoconferencing
- Webcams
- Blogs
- Social networking

Case study: Estate agent

A typical small independent estate agent sells properties in the local area and has a commercial property department dealing with property such as restaurants, shops and warehouses.

The company also represents the builders of various new housing estates in the area and the re-selling of houses as people move on. With large numbers of the local population commuting to neighbouring towns there is often a thriving market in the agency's property rental and lettings division.

The company can also offer added services including conveyancing, financial advice, mortgage broking and household insurance broking.

▶ *What you will learn*

How businesses can communicate with employees and others working remotely.

Case study: Supermarket

The SaverShop supermarket has been a retailer for over 125 years and is recognised for its excellent fresh food, value for money and friendly staff. It offers competitively branded products with lots of variety, as well as its own less expensive ranges.

To try and keep ahead in the fiercely competitive retail industry, the past few years have seen the successful expansion of products to meet the varying lifestyles, locations and shopping needs of the customer.

The store tries to offer value to their customers by selling specialist products, computer games at budget prices, cheap TVs, videos and some jeans and trainers.

The shop is open six days a week from 8a.m. to 11p.m. The store also has a free special shopper and delivery service for disabled shoppers in the local area who can't get to the store.

Introduction

All businesses need to be able to communicate with their employees who work on site and remotely. Good and fast communication helps employees to carry out their job tasks more efficiently, which will make the business run smoother and make more money.

Good communication with customers is also important. The business will need to make sure that customers are aware of, for example, any special offers, new products or services being offered and to keep customer loyalty.

There are many ways in which communication can be carried out. As technology has improved, there have been many developments in communication methods over the past few years. The increased use of these methods makes sure that communication is faster and more freely available. The most important development that has helped communication is the internet. The increased use of the internet has enabled new communication technologies to be developed and used.

Communication methods and how they support businesses

There are many different ways that a business can communicate with its employees. The location of the employees does not really matter. The employees may be working in an office, 'on the road' or remotely in another location. Other people, such as customers, can also be in communication with the business – they will also be remote as far as communication methods are concerned.

The important thing to remember when selecting a communication method to use is that it must be appropriate for the person receiving the information and the type of information being sent. For example, if images are part of the information being sent then using a **voice telephone** as the communication method would not be appropriate as the images could not be seen.

Voice telephones

These can be a fixed land line or mobile phone. They enable people to talk to each other, holding a conversation. With a land line calls can only be received at a specified location – where the phone is plugged in. With a mobile phone the call can be taken anywhere as long as there is a network signal.

Key word

Voice telephone

Key words

Short message service
Electronic mail
Chat room

SMS

This is the abbreviation for **short message service**. This is a system that lets mobile phone users send and receive text messages.

Instant messaging

This is the exchange of typed messages between computer users in real time via the internet.

Email

This is the abbreviation for **electronic mail**. Email is a way that a computer user, including those using a mobile phone such as a Blackberry or iPhone, connected to the internet, can communicate with other connected users through text and send documents, images, sound and video clips as attachments.

Chat rooms

A site on the internet where a number of users can communicate in real time. **Chat rooms** are usually related to a particular topic.

3

Forums

An internet **forum**, or message board, is an online discussion site where people can hold conversations in the form of posted messages. They differ from chat rooms as the messages are not shown in real time. To be able to see new messages the forum page must be reloaded or refreshed.

Bulletin boards

An information storage system designed to allow any authorised computer user to access, view and add to it remotely.

VoIP

This is the abbreviation for **voice over internet protocol**. This is a system that allows the human voice (analogue signal) to be converted to digital so that telephone calls may be made over the internet. Phone-to-phone communication can also use this technology.

Key word

Videoconferencing

Videoconferencing

This allows people at two or more locations to communicate by simultaneous two-way video and audio transmissions.

Webcams

A camera that inputs to a computer connected to the internet, so that live streaming of images can be viewed by internet users.

Blogs

A website on which an individual or group of users record opinions or information on a regular basis.

Social networking

The use of a dedicated website to communicate informally with other members of the site, by posting messages, photographs or videos.

Advantages and disadvantages of the different types of communication methods

Communication method	Advantages	Disadvantages
Voice telephones	• Voice conversations can be held • Calls can be taken at a fixed location (land lines) or any geographic location (mobile phones) • Voicemail messages can be left • Smart/mobile phones have lots of other features (for example, pictures can be sent during a call)	• The network signal for a mobile phone may be weak or down so calls cannot be made or taken • Land line phones may not always be answered • Time differences may not be considered when making a call to a mobile phone
SMS	• It's cheap – usually included in mobile phone packages • Short messages can be sent • Can quickly connect many people around the world	• Only short messages can be sent • Can be difficult to type an SMS on a phone keypad • May not be delivered if the phone network is down
Instant messaging	• Messages are sent in real time and responses are instantaneous • Files/pictures can be sent in instant messaging conversations • It is similar to talking face-to-face to a person • It is possible to talk to many people at once	• Emotions cannot be expressed as well as they can be when actually talking to a person • People can send viruses through files/pictures
Email	• Information can be sent quickly to many people for the time it takes to email one person • Effective in providing quick answers to questions • A range of information can be sent as attachments to an email • Can be accessed using a range of devices such as smartphone, notebook or laptop as long as there is access to the internet • Employees'/customers' email addresses can be stored	• Email can become impersonal or misunderstood • Emails may get sent to the wrong person if addresses are not checked • People may not receive emails because of no internet connection/filters on email settings • Attachments can contain a virus • Email accounts can get hacked with spam being sent to all contacts
Chat rooms	• Brings people together who have an interest in a specific topic • Users may not have the opportunity to interact in the real world due to, for example, their remote location	• Information provided by users may be false/untrue • You don't know who you are talking to • Can be very addictive
Forums	• Ideas can be shared between users • Posts/threads can be read and reread	• They can be time consuming to maintain and monitor • Comments/posts are not available in real time

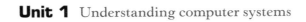

Communication method	Advantages	Disadvantages
Bulletin boards	• Any registered user can make comments which are visible to everyone immediately • Can get a fast response to a question/comment • For general discussion on topics, interesting and useful comments can be given	• Any registered user can make comments/give answers which may be incorrect • Needs to be moderated by a responsible/trustworthy person
VoIP	• With a broadband internet connection (DSL or cable), PC-to-PC phone calls are free • Calls can be made wherever there is a broadband connection by signing in to the VoIP account • Lots of features such as call forwarding, call waiting, voicemail, caller ID and three-way calling • Data, such as images and documents, can be sent, at the same time as the call is being made • Examples of VoIP services include Skype and Google Talk (these services also allow videoconferencing)	• PC-to-voice phone calls can be costly • No service during a power cut • Poor or limited internet connection can affect the quality of the sound of the call, such as voice delay, or result in dropped calls • Using a PC at the same time can reduce the quality of the call
Videoconferencing	• People don't need to travel to meetings • Fuel/travel costs reduced • Better for environment • People taking part in the conference can be at different locations • Videoconferencing can be carried out using VoIP services such as Skype and Google Talk (if the business already has these services for VoIP then the cost of equipment can be reduced)	• Time zones may be different if people are in different parts of the world • The equipment can fail or systems may crash/go offline • Training may be needed to use the equipment • Someone may need to be employed to set up and maintain the equipment • To take part in the conference everyone must have the equipment – this may be cost prohibitive
Webcams	• Webcams are used when a business is carrying out a videoconference • Allows real time and face-to-face personal interaction • When combined with a high-speed internet connection and other equipment, allows people around the country or world to see and communicate • Can reduce travel expenses and allow projects to be monitored in real time • Objects/charts can be shown	• Can be expensive to buy if advanced features are needed • Does not fully show human reactions to what is being said or shown
Blogs	• They are an easy way to keep people updated on a project • Can be used as marketing tools by businesses and to get customer/employee feedback	• Need to be moderated, which can take a lot of time • Posts are not private and information could be leaked

Communication method	Advantages	Disadvantages
Social networking	• Enables users to upload images/files to share • Connections between friends can be made • Can be used to promote a business so increasing awareness • A business can 'follow' their competitors to see what they are doing	• Lack of anonymity – some users may post too many personal details so affecting their work and private life • Can be time consuming and detract from 'normal' life • Some people can become obsessed with social networking sites • Scams and identity theft can occur

Businesses can use these communication methods to communicate with their employees and others. Which communication method is used will depend on the type of information and message that is being sent.

Activity

Choose any two of the different providers of VoIP – look on the internet to see the different providers available.

Copy and complete the following table to show the features which are available (four features have been given for you).

	Provider 1	Provider 2
Call waiting		
Call hunt		
Ring list		
3-way calling		

Activity

Research, using the internet, the developments in these communication methods.

Write a short report on how businesses are using the developments you have found in their business activities.

The estate agent could use many of these methods:

Method	Possible use(s)
Voice telephones	• To contact employees/customers quickly and, if dialling a mobile phone, wherever they are • To leave voicemail messages if the person is not available
SMS	• To pass short messages on to employees/customers. For example, confirming an appointment/sending a reminder of an appointment • To give details of new properties to employees/customers
Blogs	• To keep employees/customers informed about the building progress of a new house
Email	• To send property details to customers and employees • To keep customers informed about the sale/purchase of a house • To tell employees about new houses/properties to sell or rent • To confirm appointments with customers and employees • To send reminders to employees/customers about appointments • Distribution lists can be set up to send marketing emails to customers
Social networking	• The estate agent could have a page where information about houses/properties can be shared and comments left • A social networking microsite on an intranet to enable employees to collaborate on a project and share ideas
VoIP	• To communicate with employees who work remotely • To send brochures about houses/properties at the same time as talking to a customer • To hold a videoconference between people who are located remotely
Videoconferencing /webcams	• To communicate with builders about the progress of a new house being built • To show customers a house/property in real time

Activity

Investigate how a shop could use SMS, email and VoIP to communicate with their suppliers.

Hints and tips

You must ensure that you keep up to date with the developments in communication methods. It is important that you make sure that you know how the communication methods help support businesses, their employees and others working remotely. Exam questions might ask you about these communication methods and their advantages and disadvantages.

Exam-type questions

1 Describe **two** advantages and **one** disadvantage to the estate agent of using VoIP as a communication method. [6 marks]

2 The supermarket is considering using videoconferencing to communicate with customers. Describe **two** disadvantages to its customers. [4 marks]

3 Describe **one** advantage and **one** disadvantage of using SMS to communicate with employees. [4 marks]

Email

Introduction

Email can be a very clear method of communication. It must be used appropriately if the message is to be useful to the person receiving it.

An email is made up of two parts – the header and the body.

The email message **header** usually contains:

- From: – the email address of the sender of the email
- To: – the email address(es) of the person(s) the email is being sent to
- Subject: – a brief summary of the contents of the email
- Date: – the time and date the email was sent
- Attachment: – where any files attached are shown.

The **body** is where the actual content of the email is written.

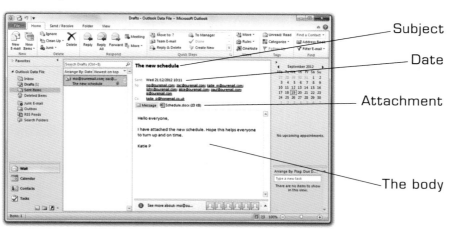

For a business to make sure that emails are opened by the person they are being sent to, it is important that the information in the header of the email is correct and appropriate.

Header information

Subject line

The **subject line** is important as it gives the person receiving the email an idea of what the email is about. A subject line should always be included when an email is being written. The subject should be meaningful and, if possible, give a description of what the email is about.

For example, if the estate agent is emailing a customer about a house, the subject line:

`'A house'`

would not be very meaningful. The subject line:

`'House for sale - Cambridge area'`

would enable the customer to know that the email contains information about a house for sale in the Cambridge area.

By using a sensible subject line a business can be more confident that the email will be opened and read. If a subject line is not included in the email header then many spam filters will consider it to be 'junk email' and will either delete the email or move it to a junk email box where it may be automatically deleted. This would be bad for a business as it means that the email would not be read.

Cc and Bcc

Cc stands for **carbon copy**. This means that everyone who is sent the email will receive it and be able to see who else was sent the email. For example, a business may want to copy someone in for information only.

Bcc stands for **blind carbon copy**. This is the same as Cc but it means that the people who were sent the email will not be shown in the header. This can be used if an email needs to be sent to lots of people but the sender does not want email addresses to be seen or for anyone to know who else has been sent the email. Another example of the use of Bcc may be when information is being sent to a group of customers but each customer's address needs to be kept private. Bcc could also be used by a business to keep an audit trail of emails.

Attachments

Attachments are files that are sent with an email. An attachment will increase the size of an email and could make an email slow to send. Most attachments are acceptable but some can contain a virus. Opening an attachment without virus checking it first can lead to a computer, or other email-receiving device such as a smartphone or tablet, being

Key words

Spyware
Email etiquette
Address book

infected with a virus or **spyware**. Attachments can be blocked or returned if the receiving email systems consider them to be dangerous. Some attachments may not be able to be read by the receiver. This may be because the receiver may not have the correct software installed on the receiving device. This may be important in business where specialised software is used. If a business is sending attachments to a customer they should check that the attachments can be opened. One way around this issue could be to provide a weblink within the body of the email which could then be used to either access the correct software or the attachment being sent.

It is always a good idea, when sending an attachment with an email, to mention in the email body that there are file(s) attached. This is just in case the file(s) does not get attached or does not get received.

Email etiquette

Email is a very useful communication tool but there are some rules (netiquette) that should always be followed. Some of these rules are:

- use an appropriate subject line
- follow the agreed email policy within the business
- check the message content before hitting the send button
- include a signature on any business emails
- do be polite
- messages should be written in plain English with careful use of abbreviations
- do not write the message in capital letters
- check if the email should be replied to all the sending list or just the person the email was originally from
- tell people the format of any attachments you send if they're anything other than standard. For example, Microsoft Office file types.

Address book(s)

An email **address book** can be very useful in business. An address book is where all email addresses and other contact details such as mobile phone numbers can be stored. Each entry about a person is called a contact. The information stored about a contact can be edited if any of the details change.

Activity

Your school may have an email policy. Find the policy and identify any rules of **email etiquette** which are included or missing.

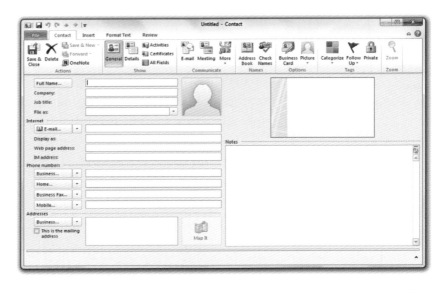

A business could ask customers for their email addresses to enable them to be contacted. In a business this could be used to contact customers, for example, if there was a special offer, to confirm details of an appointment or to send out advertising leaflets using an attachment.

Different lists can be set up within an address book.

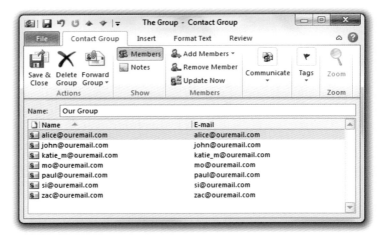

For example, the estate agents could set up a list of all the customers interested in buying or renting a shop.

Most businesses will also have an internal list with the email addresses of staff who work for them. This will allow all employees to access internal email addresses.

Activity

Many businesses send emails with signatures to show who the email has been sent from. Investigate different email signatures from different businesses – what do they include and why?

Hints and tips

It is important that you make sure that you know how email can be used appropriately by businesses. You must also know the advantages and disadvantages of email. Exam questions may ask you about the appropriate use of email and the advantages and disadvantages.

Specification coverage

Diary management
software:
- Creating appointments/
  meetings
- Inviting participants
- Creating tasks
- Creating to-do lists
- Setting reminders

What you will learn

How diary management
software can be used to
organise work schedules.

Key word

**Diary management software
(DMS)**

Exam-type questions

1 Describe when Bcc could be used when a business is sending an email.   [2 marks]

2 Describe **two** benefits to the estate agent of sending attachments
to its customers.   [2 marks]

3 Explain why an estate agent might want to set up a customer email
distribution list.   [2 marks]

4 Describe **one** advantage and **one** disadvantage to the estate agent
of setting up distribution lists.   [4 marks]

Diary management software
Introduction

Diary management software (DMS) can be very useful to employees
who work remotely. Using DMS, employees who work in an office and
those who work remotely are able to co-ordinate their diaries to ensure
that everyone who is needed can attend an appointment/meeting.

DMS also enables employees who are working on the same project,
to plan and track the progress of the project, to allocate tasks to
different members of the team and to share files and documents that
are needed during the project.

By installing and using DMS, a business can ensure that all employees
are able to communicate with each other to make sure that all tasks are
completed, appointments/meetings do not clash and reminders are set to
make sure that meetings/appointments are not missed.

Diary management software tasks

Diary management software (DMS) lets users organise work
schedules by completing the following tasks within their job role:

- **Create appointments/meetings** – DMS will allow the creation
  and storage of a list of appointments and who will be attending. The
  DMS may also show any clashes between appointments/meetings
  and may suggest alternative times.
- **Invite participants** – when an appointment/meeting has been created,
  DMS will be able to invite, by email, the people who need to attend it.
- **Create tasks/projects** – DMS can provide a task list which could
  include who is to complete each task and the deadline for each task.
  The priority of the tasks can also be set. The deadline and priority of
  each task can be changed. Some DMS can allow users to set tasks for
  others. Task lists can be shared by many users and can control which
  users have access to the lists. Task lists can be set up for individuals
  or projects or anything that needs doing.

■ **Create to-do lists** – these are very similar to tasks/projects but are usually small tasks which need to be completed and could be used as reminders. Some users of DMS may use the to-do list facility to create personal lists. For example, make a dentist appointment, buy a birthday present or take the dog to the vets.

■ **Set reminders** – a DMS can automatically remind people of an appointment/meeting they have to attend. Reminders can be set to activate at different times prior to the appointment/meeting. For example, 1 hour or 30 minutes before the start time. Reminders can also be attached to tasks, and the people who need to complete the tasks.

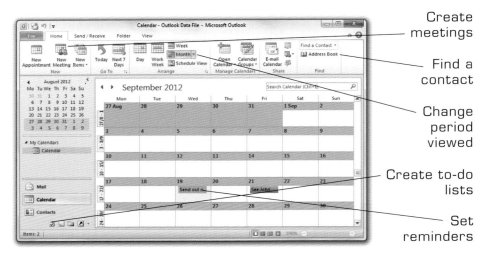

Create meetings

Find a contact

Change period viewed

Create to-do lists

Set reminders

Key word

Mobile application (app)

DMS can allow users to share their diaries with other employees or keep some things private.

Many DMS systems are now cloud software applications. This means that the DMS can be accessed through a web browser or mobile application. A **mobile application** or mobile **app** is a software application, such as DMS, which is usually designed to run on smartphones (for example an iPhone or Android) and tablet computers (for example an iPad). Some mobile apps can be downloaded to less mobile computers such as laptops or desktop PCs.

The DMS would be stored and accessed through servers at a remote location to the business – the cloud. Changes made to the DMS and files that need to be accessed by users are also stored on these servers.

This would be useful for employees who work remotely. These employees would be able to access the DMS wherever they are through the use of a mobile app. This would enable them to schedule any appointments and see what appointments/meetings are already scheduled. They would also be able to access their task list if they are working with others on a project. Any files and documents that would

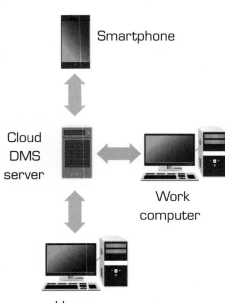

Smartphone

Cloud DMS server

Work computer

Home computer

be needed to complete any tasks set could also be accessed through the DMS and the cloud environment.

It is possible for DMS to show the appointments/meetings for a single person or a group of people. If the appointments/meetings are shown for a group of people then DMS can be closed or open.

This means that it is possible for just those people who have the access logins and passwords to access the DMS (closed) or those with the address (open). Different access rights would be granted depending on whether the access is closed or open.

For example, if closed access was granted then these people would be able to view, add or amend the facilities of the DMS. Those with open access would only be allowed to view the DMS. This access could be useful if, for example, a builder of a new property wanted to see when an employee of the estate agents was available for a site visit.

Exam-type questions

1 Describe how diary management software (DMS) could be used when arranging a meeting between the shop managers in the supermarket. [2 marks]

2 Explain how diary management software (DMS) could help a team of employees of the estate agent who are working on the same project. [6 marks]

Hints and tips

You must ensure that you are able to explain how diary management software (DMS) can be used to organise work schedules. It is important that you know how the appropriate use of DMS can be used to support business working practices. Exam questions may ask you to explain the features of DMS and how these can be used in business.

▶ *Specification coverage*

Creating and editing documents collaboratively:
- Documents in shared access locations, that is:
  - ➤ Network shared areas (for example, read/write access)
  - ➤ Cloud-based services (for example, providing open – or restricted – access to services enabling the creating/editing of documents online)
- Inserting comments into an existing draft
- Editing drafts, tracking changes made
- Reviewing facilities: accepting or rejecting changes made

▶ *What you will learn*

How documents can be created and edited collaboratively.

Creating and editing documents

Introduction

All businesses create documents. The documents that could be created by a business include:
- letters
- leaflets/brochures
- websites
- reports
- presentations
- memos
- invoices
- order forms.

These may be for internal or external use. Documents can also be classed as formal or informal.

An internal document will usually be seen only by those employees who work for the business. An external document will usually be seen by employees, customers of the business and the general public.

A formal document, such as a letter, will have a formal layout/structure and use formal language and words. An informal document will have a less structured layout/structure and will use a less formal style of writing.

Documents in shared access areas

It is sometimes necessary for business documents, such as a report or PowerPoint presentation, to be created by a group, or team, of employees. The employees may not all be based in the same location. This means that all employees working on the document will need to have access.

There are two different ways in which documents can be stored in a shared access location.

1 Shared areas on the business computer network which will allow all team members to have access to the documents being worked on. Different access levels can be set so that some members of the team can write and edit the documents whilst other will only be able to read the documents.

2 Cloud-based services which will allow all team members to access documents online. The access can be open or restricted so that documents can be created and edited online. This means that if members of the team are in different locations they can all still work collaboratively on the documents.

Inserting comments into an existing draft document

The ability to insert comments into an existing draft can be very useful when reviewing a document.

If more than one person is involved in the creation of a document, then inserting comments is an easy and effective way to collaborate. Comments about a draft document can be inserted without having to print a paper copy and add comments to it.

If a comment is added then it can be read and deleted with no action, or, where appropriate, the comments can be incorporated into the document. The initials of the reviewer making the comments can be seen in the comment box. This means that if several people have made comments it is possible to see who 'said what'.

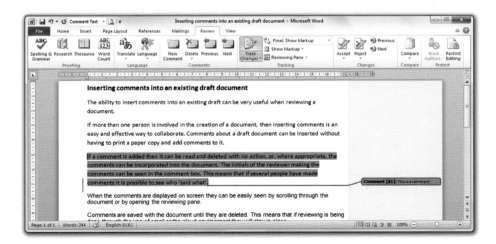

When the comments are displayed on screen they can be easily seen by scrolling through the document or by opening the reviewing pane.

Comments are saved with the document until they are deleted. This means that if reviewing is being done through the use of email or the cloud environment they will stay in place.

Editing and track changes

Documents can be reviewed and edited using the track changes facility. By using the track changes facility in a word processing program the changes that are made by another person can be seen. The changes are usually highlighted in a different colour to the original text with the changes that have been made also shown in a reviewing pane.

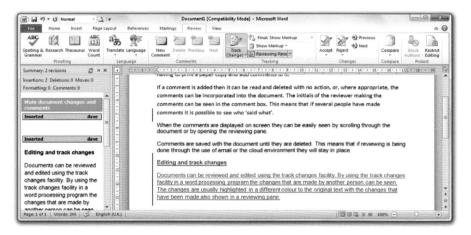

The word processing program will insert marks and details that show where deletions, insertions and formatting changes have been made. This is known as 'the markup' version of the document.

It is possible that documents will be reviewed by more than one person. The track changes facility will allow many different people to review a document and make changes to it.

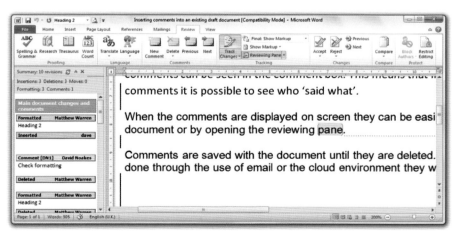

If many people have reviewed the document then some word processing programs will enable the creator of the document to see each reviewer's changes and any comments made, separately.

Reviewing facilities, accepting or rejecting changes made

Each suggested change (revision) made and tracked can be accepted or rejected by the creator of the document. If a document is being written collaboratively then there may be no one creator of the document. In this case, some form of procedure should be followed to ensure that the reviewing process is managed by one person who has overall control. The other people involved in creating the document should be able to see and check any revisions made. Changes can be dealt with one at a time or all at once. Comments can be read, actioned if appropriate and then deleted.

As changes are accepted or rejected and comments are deleted, the markup that indicates the changes and comments is removed from the document. Accepted changes become part of the document when it is saved.

Exam-type questions

1 An employee of the estate agent has created a draft of an advertising brochure for a house for sale. Describe how the comment facility could be used during the production process of the brochure. [4 marks]

2 An employee of the supermarket has created a word-processed report. The report is being sent to the supermarket manager so that it can be checked and improvements recommended. Identify and describe **two** reviewing facilities benefits that the shop manager could use to complete this task. [4 marks]

Hints and tips

You must ensure that you are able to explain how documents can be created and edited collaboratively. It is important that you know how the appropriate use of the editing tools can be used to support business working practices. It is important that you make sure that you know how the tools which can be used to create and edit documents collaboratively can help employees. Exam questions may ask you to explain the appropriate use of these tools.

4

How legal, ethical, safety and security issues affect how computers should be used

Case study: Dental surgery

Ben's Dental Surgery has a staff of four dentists and two dental nurses. There is also a receptionist who makes the appointments for the patients. The bookings are done on a computer with the personal details of the patients also held on the computer system.

The surgery is open five days a week and also offers an emergency out-of-hours service for patients.

The surgery has toilet facilities, a local advertisement board (which is free to all) and TVs in the waiting and surgery rooms.

A retail counter in the reception area sells a wide range of dental and dental hygiene products, such as toothbrushes, toothpaste and mouthwash.

Case study: Supermarket

The SaverShop supermarket has been a retailer for over 125 years and is recognised for its excellent fresh food, value for money and friendly staff.

To try and keep ahead in the fiercely competitive retail industry, the past few years have seen the successful expansion of products to meet the varying lifestyles, locations and shopping needs of the customer.

The store tries to offer value to their customers by selling specialist products, computer games at budget prices, cheap TVs, videos and some jeans and trainers.

The shop is open six days a week from 8a.m. to 11p.m. The store also has a free special shopper and delivery service for disabled shoppers in the local area who can't get to the store.

▶ **Specification coverage**

- Health and safety
- Data protection
- Copyright
- Computer misuse

▶ **What you will learn**

How legislation affects
business computer users.

Legislation

Introduction

Most businesses use computers to enable their business to run smoothly. Amongst the tasks which are carried out using computers are:

- storing personal data on employees and customers
- creation of business documents
- stock control
- finance tasks such as invoicing, ordering and maintaining the financial accounts of the business.

As many of the computers used in business are connected to the internet, many businesses worry that others will misuse their computers by, for example, stealing business data to commit fraud.

Over the years, a number of laws have been passed to make misusing computers to do harm to others, steal their ideas or their data, or to reveal information about others illegal. These laws do not stop people misusing computers, but they can act as a deterrent to try and prevent computer misuse. The laws also give the victims of computer crime some way of recovering any losses they may have suffered.

There are four main areas of laws that relate to the use of computers in the United Kingdom:

- Health and safety
- Data protection
- Copyright
- Computer misuse.

Organisations are required to comply with all relevant laws affecting how computers are used in the workplace. They are also required to know about any changes to legislation, for example the introduction of new laws and how these might affect how business users of computers should behave. What follows is a discussion of the main laws in these areas affecting business organisations in 2012.

Hints and tips

The specification does not list specific laws that you should know about in detail. You will be tested on your understanding of how business users are affected by laws covering health and safety, data protection, copyright and computer misuse. Like business organisations, you should have an awareness of the relevant legislation, including any changes after this book was published.

Health and safety

Almost everyone, not just all employees and employers, has a duty under the Health and Safety at Work Act to work and behave safely. The Act also makes it illegal to act recklessly or intentionally act in such a way as to endanger yourself or others. Employees must take reasonable care for their own and others safety and cooperate with their employers in doing so.

The Act applies to those using computers for their work but not necessarily to those using them at home, unless the employee works at home.

The main law covering the use of computer equipment is the Health and Safety (Display Screen Equipment) Regulations. These state that employers (a business) have to do five main tasks to ensure the safety of their employees:

1 Analyse workstations and assess and reduce risks

Employers need to check that the computer equipment and the area around it are safe. If any risks are found during the assessment of the workstation and surrounding area then action needs to be taken to make them safe.

2 Ensure that workstations meet the minimum requirements

Employers need to make sure that adjustable chairs and suitable lighting are provided for employees. Tilt and swivel monitors should also be provided and the workstation should have sufficient space for the keyboard, monitor and any paperwork needed by the employee.

3 Plan work so that there are breaks or changes of activity

Employees should not be expected to work at a computer all day. Regular breaks should be provided or a change in the activity that the employees are carrying out. However, the regulations do not say how long or how frequent the breaks should be.

4 Arrange and pay for eye tests and glasses (if special ones are needed)

Employees of a business, who are covered by these regulations, can ask that eye tests are arranged and paid for. The eye tests can be repeated as advised by the optician – the business will have to keep paying for these. The business will only have to pay for glasses if special ones are required.

Activity

Investigate the health and safety policy, which applies to computer systems users, at your centre. Write down the main points of the policy and summarise how the computer users are affected by the policy.

5 Provide health and safety training and information

Employers must provide training to make sure that their employees can use their computer equipment and workstations correctly. The training they provide could include how employees can use the equipment to minimise risks to their health. Employers should also provide information to their employees about health and safety when using screen equipment and the steps that have been taken to minimise the risks.

Health problems

It would, however, be very silly not to take care when using computers at home as prolonged use of computers may damage your health. There are a number of conditions that may be caused by long periods of use of computers.

RSI

Repetitive strain injury (RSI) may be caused by the repetitive clicking of the buttons of a mouse or using a keyboard and shows itself as pain in the arms. The pain gets worse with any activity and the area affected may be weak. It is not certain that RSI is actually caused by repetitive actions when using computers but these actions do seem to make the condition worse.

Headaches

Headaches are often caused by problems with vision and having a computer monitor too far away, too dim or too bright, or having the text on the screen at the wrong size.

Neck and back pain

Neck or back pain may be associated with incorrect posture. Sitting at the wrong height, or wrong distance or for long periods at computer desks may cause back or neck pain. Using a proper 'computer chair' such as one that provides proper back support and is adjustable will lower the risk of back pain or damage. Also, having computer monitors at the wrong distance or angle may cause neck or back pain.

Eye strain

Eye strain or sore eyes may be caused by using computers for long periods. Staring at a computer screen for long periods without blinking will cause the eye to dry out; having the wrong size text on screen will strain the eyes when trying to read it; having too bright or dim colours will cause eye strain; and not setting the resolution of the monitor appropriately will strain the eyes. Another consideration is the light level and reflections for monitors as these can affect how easily the work on the screen is seen. Using computers will not damage your eyes but might make them sore or cause headaches.

Activity

Investigate each health problem shown in the following table and complete the other columns.

Health problem	Description	Cause	Possible action needed
RSI			
Headaches			
Neck and back pain			
Eye strain			

Physical safety

Using computers can also cause physical problems for employees. Employees should make sure that they:

- use a proper office chair with proper back support and adjustable height (the chair should have a single, central leg that allows the chair to swing around and that leg should have at least five supporting points, ideally each with a wheel so that the chair can move easily)
- do not drink or eat when using a computer due to the possible electrical hazards, and the possible spillage of food and drink into the computer itself!
- do not tamper with any cables or computer parts
- place the computer equipment safely so it cannot fall or be knocked over
- take care of their own health and safety and that of others.

Data Protection Act

The Data Protection Act (DPA) aims to protect the rights of the owners of data. It does not actually protect the data. The Act sets out rules on how data should be stored and used, and provides a means for the owners of data to complain and sometimes to claim compensation if their data is misused.

Activity

Create a list of the dos and dont's for an ICT room in your centre.

Key terms related to the DPA

Term	Explanation
Personal data	Any information about a living individual, which might include both facts and opinions, that includes sufficient information to allow the individual to be identified. Facts include name, address and date of birth. Other examples of facts about an individual could include qualifications gained, medical history and known allergies. Details that contain name and date of birth would be considered personal data whilst statistics collected from a questionnaire completed anonymously, without any details such as name or address, would not.
Data subject	The person about who the data is being stored.
Data user	The person who needs to access or use the data as part of their job.
Data controller	This is the person who needs to apply for permission to collect and store data. The data controller is often the person in charge of the business but sometimes a different person who works in the business may have this responsibility. This person decides what data needs to be collected and what it will be used for and how.
Information Commissioner	This is the person who enforces the Data Protection Act and who organisations need to apply to in order to gain permission to collect and store personal data.

Key words

Data subject
Data user
Data controller
Information Commissioner

Storing data on computers makes it easier for that data to be accessed and used by the business, but it can also make the data more available to those who would misuse it.

The Data Protection Act tries to protect individuals by giving them rights to access any data stored by others and to try and make sure that the data is processed appropriately. Most people would prefer that their personal data is kept private and cannot be accessed or used by everyone.

The DPA gives everyone the right to know what data is stored about them on a business computer system and the right to see it. If someone feels that they are not being allowed to see their personal data being stored, or feel that the data is not being processed properly, they can contact the government Information Commissioner's Office and ask for help. The Information Commissioner's Office will investigate the matter and if necessary can take action against the business.

How personal data should be handled

The DPA lays down eight principles about how personal data should be handled by anyone storing the data:

1 Personal data must be fairly and lawfully processed

This means that personal data must not be collected by misleading the person into providing it and that the personal data collected can only be used lawfully.

2 Personal data must be processed for limited purposes

This means that personal data must only be used for the purpose for which it was obtained. For example, a person's email address collected so that a business can reply to enquiries must not be used, without the person's permission, for any other purpose such as email marketing.

3 Personal data must be adequate, relevant and not excessive

This means that personal data that is stored should be just enough for the task to be carried out, only relevant to the task, and should not include other data. For example, a bank would only need to hold a customer's name and address, for example, and not any details of their qualifications.

4 Personal data must be accurate and up to date

This means the person storing the data has a duty to ensure that any data they hold is accurate and free from errors. This is the principle that most people worry about because inaccurate data stored by, for example, their bank, can cause many difficulties. Most people who ask to see the data held about them are concerned that the business holds data that is not accurate and want to get it corrected.

5 Personal data must not be kept for longer than is necessary

Data should be destroyed/deleted when it is no longer needed. However, this should be carried out so as to make sure that others cannot read or access the deleted data.

6 Personal data must be processed in line with your rights

This principle ensures that a person's data is processed so that their rights are respected.

7 Personal data must be kept secure

Any stored data must be kept secure. The DPA ensures that businesses that hold data must take precautions against its loss, unauthorised access and damage. The Act does not define the measures that must be taken, but this principle means that a business must take proper security measures to protect the data. For example, a business could set passwords, levels of access and use physical methods of protecting their data.

Activity

The dentist holds records about its patients including personal details. Make a list of the types of data that the dentist could keep about its patients. Do not list the actual data but write down items such as:

- Name
- Date of birth

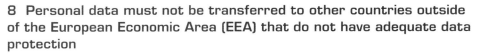

8 Personal data must not be transferred to other countries outside of the European Economic Area (EEA) that do not have adequate data protection

Other countries around the world may not have the same level of data protection as the UK, so the Act states that personal data must not be sent to countries with levels of data protection lower than those in the UK.

Copyright, Design and Patents Act

This Act (law) was first introduced in 1988 and makes it illegal to copy a work, for example, a file or image, without permission from the owner or copyright holder. It is also illegal to make unauthorised copies of software. People and businesses that break this law risk having to pay a large fine.

There are three main ways in which this law is most commonly broken:

1 Using software without the correct software licence

For example, if a piece of software has been bought by a business with a licence to install it on three PCs but the business then installs it on four PCs – then they have broken this law.

2 Downloading files from the internet

If text, images and other files are downloaded and used then permission from the copyright holder must be obtained. The name of the copyright holder should also be acknowledged. Sometimes the copyright holder may charge a fee for using their work.

3 Copying music, DVDs, CDs and software

Any copying or sharing of digital files that you have not created yourself, copying and sharing MP3 files made from music CDs and copying movies from DVDs are all breaches of copyright. If a copy of a software CD is made and then installed on a PC then this is also illegal under the Copyright, Designs and Patents Act.

Copyright lasts for many years after the initial publication of a work but only gives limited protection to the person/people who created it. Owning the copyright to a piece of work will not stop others from copying it but allows the owner to bring action in the courts. A problem is that often the person copying the work cannot be traced. This is particularly a problem with computer software, images and other digital data. For example, audio and video files where copies are easily made and shared.

Key words

Computer Misuse Act
Hacking

Computer Misuse Act

This Act relates to illegal access to files and data stored on computer systems. It was introduced to cope with the increase in **hacking** and viruses. There are three main parts to this Act (law):

1 Unauthorised access to computer material

This means that any access to materials that you do not have permission to view is against this law, as is using a computer to access data or programs stored on another computer. This is often what people refer to as 'hacking'. Hacking is only illegal if you do not have permission to access the data or use the computer to access the data.

2 Unauthorised access with intent to commit or facilitate the commission of further offences

This means that accessing computer material and then intending to use the information to commit further offences is against the law. If you access information (even if you have permission to do so) with the intention of using it to commit fraud or blackmail, for example, you are breaking this law.

3 Unauthorised acts with intent to impair or with recklessness as to impairing the operation of a computer

This means that any unauthorised alterations made to computer materials are against this law. So, if files or data are changed when you do not have permission, then this is breaking this law. For example, if you access someone else's computer files and change the contents, then you are breaking this law. Also, unauthorised altering of files to make the computer malfunction, alter how it works or damage other data also breaks this law – so sending a virus is against this law.

Penalties for breaking this law can be a prison term of several years, or fines, or both.

Hints and tips

You must ensure that you keep up to date with the developments in the legislation as the acts can be updated or replaced by new laws. You should be able to apply the legislation to a given scenario. It is important that you make sure that you know that exam questions may ask you about how the legislation affects business computer users.

Exam-type questions

1 Explain the actions that would need to be taken by the supermarket to make sure that the work stations used by its employees meet the requirements of the Health and Safety Act. [4 marks]

2 The dentist holds personal details of its patients on a computer.

a) Name the Act that relates to a business holding personal details. [1 mark]

b) Explain how this Act limits how the dentist can use the patient's personal details. [4 marks]

3 State **two** security precautions that the supermarket should take to protect the email addresses of its customers. [2 marks]

4 The supermarket is creating a flyer to tell customers about its latest offers. An image has been found on another supermarket's website.

a) State the Act that should be complied with if this image is to be used in the flyer. [1 mark]

b) State **two** actions that supermarket must take if this image is to be used in the flyer. [2 marks]

> **Specification coverage**

- The use and abuse of personal and private data
- Cyber bullying
- Monitoring of individuals by organisations

> **What you will learn**

How moral and ethical issues affect business computer users.

Moral and ethical issues

Introduction

The increased use of computer systems, including the internet, means that users need to be aware of moral and ethical issues. These issues can have an impact on other users and businesses. It is now important that businesses and employees need to consider the actions they take when using computer systems.

The use and abuse of personal and private data

Computer systems are increasingly used to hold personal and private data. Almost every business will hold data on its customers and employees. What sort of data is held will depend on the type of business. For example, the dentist's surgery may hold medical data about its patients whilst the shop may hold email addresses and contact details (for example, name and address).

The use of personal and private data, which is held on a computer system, is governed by legislation. The main Act is the Data Protection Act (DPA). The DPA governs how collected data can be used and the actions that can be taken by data subjects if their data is abused.

The Computer Misuse Act (CMA) can also deter people trying to abuse personal and private data. The CMA makes it illegal to hack into a computer system and steal the data that is stored on it. If a computer

system is hacked into and personal and private data stolen then this can have a huge impact on the people and the business who the data relates to.

Sometimes the employees of a business can accidently abuse personal and private data. It is possible that files are not saved as edits when changes are being made. For example, if a customer provides updated contact details and these are not saved then there could be a huge impact on the business and the customer. By not saving the file then the employee is breaking one of the DPA principles – data must be accurate and up to date.

Employees could also overwrite, or delete, a file of personal and private data – this again would mean that the personal and private data has been abused. Most businesses have a policy of how to name files. This means that every file is saved with a file name which would enable anyone else working in the business to know what is in the file. A policy such as this can stop any personal and private data being 'lost'.

The abuse of personal and private data can also include employees, and other people, stealing the data. This could lead to issues such as identity theft. Identity theft means that someone else takes over that persons identity and can lead to many problems. It has been known for data to be stolen and used by criminals to commit crimes using someone else's name. This can also happen if business data is stolen.

Another way in which personal and private data could be abused is by employees damaging or destroying files. This may be because they are about to be made redundant or have a grudge against their employer. Employees could also leak user IDs and passwords to enable someone else to access the files of personal and private data.

Files can be hacked into. The **hacker** could steal a business's data and sell it to another business. The data could be damaged or deleted to harm the business. These actions are illegal under the CMA. The hacker may use the personal and private data they access to commit fraud.

The legislation was introduced to attempt to keep personal and private data from being abused. The legislation does not stop people using and abusing personal and private data but, if they are found, they can be punished.

Cyber bullying

Cyber bullying is when one person or a group of people try to threaten or embarrass someone else using technology such as a mobile phone or the internet. It can be just as bad as bullying in the real world

Activity

Create a file naming policy for use in your school.

Key word

Hacker
Cyber bullying

Activity

Investigate cyber bullying. Create some rules related to cyber bullying which could be included in a business IT policy.

but, because of the use of the internet, any embarrassing or horrid comments can be spread around the world in a matter of hours.

Cyber bullying can be carried out by people of all ages, at school or in the workplace. It is important that a business recognises the importance of attempting to stop any employees carrying out cyber bullying and it should have a section in its IT policy to cover this.

Monitoring of individuals by organisations

Some businesses may need to monitor the tasks that are being completed. This does not mean that employees are being 'watched' all the time, but some tasks could be critical to the running of the business and so need to be monitored. Another reason employees may be monitored is for an audit trail. There are several ways in which employees and other individuals (for example, customers) can be monitored.

Worker monitoring/logging

Workers (employees) of a business can be monitored (logged) in lots of different ways. One way is through the use of CCTV cameras. These are cameras that are installed and can be used to monitor and record what employees are doing. The main worry that employees may have about CCTV is an invasion of their privacy as they are being monitored at all times. The business may say that the CCTV cameras are there to protect its employees and also to protect the premises at night whilst no one should be there. There are some places where CCTV cameras should not be installed, for example, in the toilets used by employees and other people visiting the business premises.

Employees can also be monitored though the use of swipe or RFID ID cards to open doors within the premises. These cards allow different access rights to each area. For example, the office of the managing director could be restricted to themselves and other senior managers within the business. The use of these cards will enable an audit trail to be created to show who went into each area of the premises and when. This again could be seen as an invasion of privacy but the business could say that it is for the safety and security of its employees, premises and confidential information.

Activity

Investigate other methods that could be used by a business to restrict access to different areas within their premises.

Cookies

A **cookie** is a 'text file' that can be read using a program such as Notepad in the Windows operating system. The file usually contains two pieces of information: a site name and unique user ID.

When a website is first accessed a cookie can be downloaded onto the computer system. The next time the website is accessed the computer system checks to see if it has a cookie that is relevant (that is, one containing the site name) and sends the information contained in that cookie back to the website.

The website then 'knows' that the website has been accessed before and can personalise what appears on the screen. This personalisation will continue to take place every time that the website is accessed.

Some cookies are able to record how long is spent on each page of the website, what links are clicked and any accessibility options that are activated. Cookies can also be used to store data on what is in a 'shopping cart', adding items as the user clicks.

If the shop were to offer online shopping to its customers, then the shop's website could contain a cookie to make the task of selecting and ordering the goods to be delivered easier for their customers.

The main problem with using cookies is that some people do not like the idea of a business storing their information gathered by the cookie. Some businesses may use cookies to create a marketing list or target special offers which are relevant to website users based on their previous browsing or shopping habits.

However, the collection and storage of personal information without permission is not strictly legal in the UK. Sites that make use of cookies get around this in two ways. The terms and conditions of the website will state that by using that website a user is agreeing to download the cookies. Also, almost all web browsers provide an option to block cookies. That means users can block all cookies or can pick and choose which ones to accept.

Key logging

A **key logger** is a piece of hardware or software that records the real-time activity of a computer user including the keyboard keys they press.

Key loggers can be used in the IT department of a business to troubleshoot technical problems with a computer system. They can also be used by a business to monitor the use of a computer system by its employees without them knowing. This means that an audit trail of any websites visited or keys pressed on a keyboard will be recorded.

Key loggers can also be used by criminals on public computers to steal passwords or credit card information.

Key logger software is freely available on the internet. They allow keystrokes to be captured but can also collect screen captures (prints) from a computer system. Normal key logging software stores data on the local/network hard drive, but some can automatically transmit data over the network to a remote computer or web server.

Detecting the presence of a key logger on a computer system can be difficult but anti-key logging software is available.

Worker call monitoring/recording

Many businesses will record telephone calls made from and to the business. This enables an audit trail to be kept in case of any issues or questions that may be raised at a later date. For example, the dentist surgery may record any calls made to patients about test results just in case the patient has further questions or queries about the call.

Calls can also be recorded by a business for training purposes. Some calls made to or from a business may be complicated and these can be used to assist in training employees in how to deal with these situations and problems.

Some businesses may have a policy about private phone calls made during working hours and so monitoring phone calls made could assist in employees keeping to the terms of this policy.

Monitoring workers can have an impact on them. It may help workers keep on track with the tasks they have to complete, improve productivity and enable employers to reward those employees who are most productive. However, this may encourage some workers to work longer than they are contracted to do.

Electronic consumer surveillance

Many retail businesses offer a loyalty card scheme. Every time a customer shops at the store, online or in the store, the loyalty card number is obtained and points are allocated to the account. At regular intervals (for example, 3 or 6 monthly) points are converted into vouchers which the customer can chose to spend, save or exchange for goods or services.

This means that the business keeps track of every transaction a customer makes – including what is bought and where. This allows the business to target different offers to different groups of customers. For example, if the card shows that the customer buys dog feed every week then targeted offers about dog food may be sent to the customer.

It is not just the business that issues the loyalty card that uses the information but many businesses are linked to others – as affiliates. The issuing business will share information with its affiliates who will then use the information to target specific marketing information.

Activity

Choose any two of the different providers of loyalty card schemes – look on the internet to see the different providers available.

Make a list to show the different rewards that customers can receive. Explain why businesses are keen to introduce loyalty schemes.

Key word

Mobile phone positioning

Activity

Research mobile phone positioning. Create a list of the advantages and disadvantages of using this method.

Mobile phone positioning

Mobile phone positioning is a method used to obtain the current position of a mobile phone (the phone can be moving or not). The method uses a minimum of three mobile phone masts to calculate the position. GPS, which you learnt about in Chapter 1, can also be used for positioning.

Mobile phone positioning can be used by the emergency services (police, fire, ambulance, coastguard or mountain rescue) to find the exact location that a call was made. This is a positive use of mobile phone positioning.

However, finding the position of a mobile phone, and the person using it, can invade the privacy of the phone user. This process allows someone to check where a person is without the person's consent.

Hints and tips

You must ensure that you know about the moral and ethical issues that can affect business computer users. You should be able to consider the issues from the point of view of employees and the business. Exam questions may ask you about these issues.

Exam-type questions

1 Describe how the supermarket could use cookies to monitor visitors to its website. [4 marks]

2 Explain how a loyalty card scheme could help the supermarket in monitoring its customers. [4 marks]

What you will learn

The implications and consequences for businesses of data loss, corruption and theft.

Data loss, corruption and theft

Introduction

A business will rely on the data it stores and processes to keep the business running. If the data that is held on the computer system is lost, corrupted or stolen then this can have a serious impact on the running of the business.

Legal implications

As you have already seen in the first part of this chapter, there are different pieces of legislation that apply to data and computer systems.

The main legislation that relates to data is the Data Protection Act (DPA). If data is lost by a business or stolen in some way, for example by a hacker, the Information Commissioner can take action against the business. One of the principles of the DPA is that personal data must be kept secure. If the data is lost or stolen then this principle has been broken. A business can have criminal proceedings started against it by the Information Commissioner and may have to pay financial compensation to any person whose data has been lost or stolen.

If data has been stolen through hacking then the legislation that can be used is the Computer Misuse Act (CMA). If the hacker is traced, then the business can allow the police to prosecute them. This could result in the hacker being imprisoned and having to pay a large fine. In addition, the hacker may also have to pay compensation to the business.

Activity

Investigate how the loss, corruption and theft of data is covered by the DPA, CMA and Copyright, Design and Patents Act.

You should think about the actions that can be taken and the penalties that would need to be faced or paid.

Impact on customers

Most businesses hold personal data about their customers. For example, the dentist surgery will hold personal details about all of its patients – some of this data may be sensitive.

If the personal data of the customers is lost, stolen or corrupted then this can have a serious impact on the customer and the business.

It is very likely that the business will no longer be seen as trustworthy by its customers and the confidence that the customers

Activity

Investigate what could happen if a person's identity were to be stolen.

had in the business will reduce. This could lead to customers moving their custom to a different business. This could lead to the business stopping trading. For example, if the shop held details of the customers who use the delivery service and this data was lost, stolen or corrupted, then the customer may find another shop to do their deliveries.

If personal data is lost, stolen or corrupted then there is an increased risk of the customers being the victims of identity theft. This means that someone takes over the identity of another person. The impact of this happening to someone can be very serious. If a person's identity is stolen then this can result in, for example, big debts being run up in their name or passports being issued and possibly being used for criminal activities.

Impact on employees

If data was to be lost, stolen or corrupted as a result of actions by an employee then there may be a great impact on the employee responsible. Most businesses have an IT policy (a business procedure) which will set down rules about data being held on the computer system and the actions that could be taken if any of these rules are broken.

An employee may face disciplinary action if their actions resulted in data being lost, stolen or corrupted. These actions could be:

- a formal written warning
- a demotion in job role and probably a reduction in salary
- dismissal from their job
- a reference being given which stated why they lost their job – this could result in difficulty in finding another job.

In addition to the actions taken against the specific employee other action may be taken. These could be an increased level of security. For example, access rights to data being changed or more monitoring of what employees are doing whilst accessing data.

Impact on the business (organisation)

The impact on a business (organisation) of having any data lost, stolen or corrupted can be very serious. Much of the legislation relating to this requires a business to pay compensation to the people whose data has been lost, stolen or corrupted. This compensation can be very high, sometimes running into thousands of pounds. If more than one person's data has been lost or stolen then this sum of money will obviously increase. The cost of compensation may result in the business having to be shut down as they do not have any money to either pay the compensation or to carry on trading.

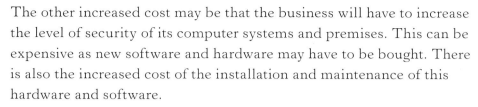
The other increased cost may be that the business will have to increase the level of security of its computer systems and premises. This can be expensive as new software and hardware may have to be bought. There is also the increased cost of the installation and maintenance of this hardware and software.

There is also a high risk that the customers of the business will lose confidence in the business and take their custom elsewhere. This can, again, lead to financial worry for the business and, without customers, they may not be able to carry on trading.

Activity

Investigate, using the internet, three UK cases where data has been lost, stolen or corrupted. Fill in the following table to show the impact on the business (organisation) and its customers of data lost, stolen or corrupted.

Name of organisation/ business	What data was lost, stolen or corrupted	How this happened	The impact on the business/ organisation	The impact on the customers

Hints and tips

You must ensure that you know about the implications and consequences for businesses and organisations of data loss, corruption and theft. You should be able to consider the legal implications of this and the impact on the customers, employees and the business. Exam questions may ask you about how data that is lost, stolen or corrupted can have an impact on customers, employees and a business, and the legal implications.

Exam-type questions

1 Describe **two** impacts to the customers of the supermarket if their data was stolen from the supermarket computer system. [4 marks]

2 Explain the legal action that could be taken if the dentist's computer system was hacked and data stolen. [4 marks]

▶ *What you will learn*

The main threats to data security and how to deal with them.

Threats to data security

Introduction

As computer systems are used to carry out more and more business activities, the threat to the computer systems has increased. The increased use of the internet as a business tool has also led to the increased risk of threats.

Businesses have to be aware of the threats to their computer systems and the impact this will have on the running of the business. It is not just the physical computer systems that need to be protected but the data held on them. As more businesses, and people, use the internet for financial transactions, for example, security of this data has to be increased to ensure that information and data does not fall into the wrong hands.

Threats to data security

Some of the most common threats to data security and computer systems are outlined in the following table:

Threat	Description
Computer virus	A computer program that can replicate itself and spread from one computer to another. Viruses can increase their chances of spreading to other computers by infecting files on a network file system or a file system that is accessed by other computers. A virus attempts to make a computer system unreliable.
Trojans	A Trojan often appears to be something which is wanted or needed by the user of a PC but is a stand-alone malicious program designed to give full control of a PC infected with a Trojan to another PC. They can be hidden in valid programs and software. Trojan horses can make copies of themselves, steal information, or harm their host computer systems.
Worm	A stand-alone computer program that replicates itself so it can spread to other computers. A worm can use a computer network to spread. Unlike a computer virus, it does not need to attach itself to an existing program. Worms almost always cause some harm to a network, even if only by consuming bandwidth.
Phishing	A way of attempting to acquire information, for example usernames, passwords and credit card details, by pretending to be from a trustworthy source such as a social network or auction site. Phishing is usually carried out by email spoofing or instant messaging. Users are often asked to enter details at a fake website which looks just like the proper version.
Spyware	A type of malware (malicious software) installed on a computer system that collects information about users without their knowledge. Spyware is usually hidden from a user and can be difficult to detect. Spyware is often secretly installed on a user's personal computer without their knowledge. However, some spyware such as key loggers may be installed to intentionally monitor users. Spyware can collect data from an infected computer, including personal information such as websites visited, user logins and financial information. Spyware can also install additional software or redirect web browsers to different websites. Some spyware can change computer settings, which could lead to slow internet connection speeds or changes in web browser settings.

Threat	Description
Adware	Also known as advertising-supported software. This is any software package that automatically shows adverts, such as a pop up. They may also be in the user interface of a software package or on an installation screen. The main object of adware is to generate revenue for its author. Adware, by itself, is harmless. However, some adware may include spyware such as key loggers.
Hacking	Hacking means finding out weaknesses in an established system and exploiting them. A computer hacker is a person who finds out weaknesses in a computer system to gain unauthorised access. A hacker may be motivated by a multitude of reasons, such as profit, protest or challenge.
Denial of service (DoS) attacks	This is an attempt to make a computer or network system unavailable to its users. A DoS attack is usually focused on preventing an internet site or service from functioning efficiently or at all, temporarily or indefinitely. The attacks usually target sites or services hosted on high-profile web servers such as banks and payment websites (for example, PayPal).
Physical threats (for example, loss/theft of devices)	Computer systems consist of physical items such as keyboards, monitors, memory sticks/removable storage devices, base units and servers. These can be lost or stolen very easily – especially memory sticks and portable storage devices.

Actions to minimise risks

There are some actions that can be taken to reduce the risks and threats of using computer systems. Some of these actions can be taken by the users of the computer systems and others can be provided by software.

Online protection

The internet is a great place to spend time – socialising with friends and shopping online as well as doing research and online banking. However, it is also a great place for criminals looking to hijack your computer, steal your identity and ultimately steal from you.

Online criminals can:

- infect a computer system with spyware to steal personal details and identities
- infect a computer system with pop ups and viruses
- take over a computer system and use it to attack other computer systems
- send spam and scam emails
- create fake websites
- hack into a network
- use email and chat to bully, con or cheat.

Businesses and people need to protect their privacy, cash, reputations and computer systems to reduce these risks. It is easier to stop a problem before it happens than try to fix it afterwards.

Sharing information

People need to be careful about the information they share about themselves online – there is no delete button on the internet.

If personal information (for example, your date of birth, your address, or dates when you are going on holiday, etc.) is posted on the internet, even if it is later deleted, there is no control over how it is stored, copied or archived.

It is not a good idea to give too much information on social networking sites (such as Facebook and MySpace) and blog sites. Identity thieves can piece together a person's identity from a variety of sources to get all the details they need.

Use different passwords for different sites

Don't use the same password across multiple websites. It is obviously more difficult to manage a number of different passwords, but it is definitely worth the effort. For example, if there is a security breach on your social networking site, it will not expose your online banking or other sensitive information if you have used different passwords for those sites.

Always check a website for the padlock symbol

If a website is being used that requires sensitive personal data to be input (address details, phone numbers, bank details, etc.) then check that a padlock symbol is displayed – this means that the information being input will be encrypted.

Beware of unsolicited/unknown senders of emails

Don't open emails where the sender's address is unknown. This type of email can contain links to code that can infect your computer. If a suspicious email is opened by mistake then any links contained in the body of the email should not be followed and the email should not be replied to.

Protection software and hardware

There are software programs and hardware devices that can be used to protect and increase the security of data. These programs and devices can be installed onto a computer system and, as long as they are used, can offer some protection against threats to data security.

Firewall

A firewall is used to help protect a computer system from threats and attacks. This is done by controlling what data can and cannot pass through it.

Activity

Investigate the advice given by social networking sites about acting safely online.

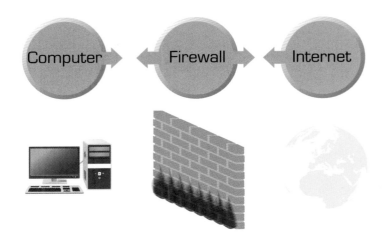

A firewall can be either software or hardware.

- **Software** – many personal computer operating systems such as Windows include software-based firewalls to protect against threats from the internet. Free firewall packages such as Comodo can be downloaded from the internet. A business may decide to buy a software firewall such as McAfee. These software packages usually include anti-virus and anti-spam software.

- **Hardware** – these boxes are much faster than software versions but they are also much more expensive and tricky to set up.

A small business network, such as the dentist, is likely to be protected by just a software firewall. However, if the business is large, or holds very sensitive data and information, for example a bank or credit card company, it is possible that they would have several hardware firewalls in addition to intruder detection software looking for unusual user and access requests.

The more valuable or sensitive the information that is held, then the higher the level of protection expected by users and the people whose information is being held.

Anti-virus software

This software detects any viruses, including Trojans and worms, and removes them to limit their damage and impact to the computer system.

The software tries to detect the virus before it enters the computer system. If a virus is detected then the software will either automatically quarantine it or will send an alert to the user asking what action should be taken. Which of these actions the software will carry out will depend on the choices selected during the installation of the **anti-virus software** package.

Key word

Anti-virus software

It is important that the anti-virus software is kept up to date. When the package is bought and installed then it will be the most up-to-date version. However, new viruses are being created and distributed all the time so the software manufacturer will release updates to reduce the risk of these new viruses.

Anti-virus scans can also be carried out by the software. These can be scheduled to automatically run at a selected time and day or can be done by a user at any time. These scans will search for any viruses that may be on the computer system and which have not been detected by the anti-virus software.

Activity

Choose any two of the different providers of anti-virus software – look on the internet to see the different providers available.

Copy and complete this table to show the features that are available. Two features have been given for you. You may need to add more rows to the table.

	Provider 1	Provider 2
Internet links scanner		
Live support		

Anti-spam software

Most anti-virus software packages also detect spam. Email spam is the electronic version of junk mail. It is the sending of unwanted messages, often unsolicited advertising, to a large number of email addresses. Spam can be a serious security concern as it can be used to deliver Trojan horses, viruses, worms, spyware and targeted phishing attacks.

Anti-spam software can be set up to detect spam emails. This can be done using the automatic setting already defined in the package or, when the software is being installed, the user can select different options.

Data encryption software

This software encrypts data so that only users who have the unlock code/secret key can read/use the data which has been transmitted.

Key word

Data encryption software

For example, a user needs to encrypt and send the phrase:

> **The cat sat on the mat**

This phrase would be received by the receiving computer system as:

> **5lgP!6n!6K*6lgB!6**

This could only be decrypted if the receiving computer system had access to the secret key. This key would, obviously, have to be kept secure and only accessed by people who were trustworthy.

Data can also be encrypted and stored/saved in an encrypted form. The secret key will be needed to unlock the data if it is to be used.

Hints and tips

You must ensure that you know about the different threats to data security and how businesses can deal with them. Exam questions may ask you about these threats and the actions that can be taken to minimise them.

Exam-type questions

1 The supermarket faces a number of threats by using the internet. Describe how phishing and Trojans are a threat to the data held on the supermarket's computer system. [4 marks]

2 The dentist needs to transfer confidential patient data by email. Describe how data encryption could be used to ensure this data is transferred securely. [3 marks]

Software updates

Introduction

It is important that software is updated. Most software vendors will make changes to the software following its release. These updates are called 'patches'. Many patches are to attempt to resolve any potential security issues that may have been identified by either the vendors or users of the software. The updating of software – operating systems and security software – can be done automatically or manually.

Automatic updates for software

Many operating systems have the facility to update automatically. This usually happen when the computer system is going through the shutdown process. When the computer system has reached a specified

(by the software vendor) point the operating system will download any updates that have become available since the last shutdown process was carried out.

At the end of the updating procedure the computer system will automatically shut down without any intervention from the user. By using the automatic updating facility the user does not have to remember to update – the computer system will automatically carry out the procedure.

Some security software will also update automatically. This process is usually completed in real time. This means that when the computer system is connected to the internet the security software will automatically be checking all the time for new updates. If an update is found then the security software will automatically download it. This happens because new viruses and other security threats covered by the software are being released all the time.

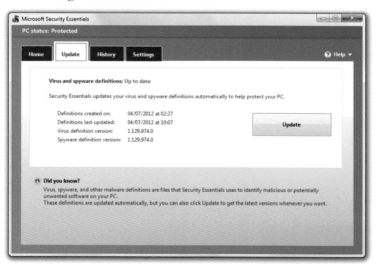

As with automatic updates for operating systems this means that the user does not have to remember to manually check for updates and so the computer system is always protected from any threats.

If a business uses automatic updates of operating systems and security software then they do not have to remember to manually check for updates and so can be sure that their computer system is as up to date as possible.

Manual updates for software

Manually updating operating systems and security software can be dangerous to the computer system and the data that is held on it. A manual update can be forgotten by an employee and this can leave the computer system vulnerable to threats.

A manual update for an operating system can be completed on an ad-hoc basis or set to be checked at a specified time by a user.

One of the problems with manual updating of software is the time it can take to download the patch. There may also be a time delay between the patch being released by the software vendor and the time when the manual update takes place.

Another problem with manually scheduling an update is that the computer system must be switched on and connected to the internet for the update to be downloaded. If the manual update is scheduled for a time when the business computer system is switched off then the business will never get updates and patches downloaded. This can leave the computer system open to attacks and threats and could result in data being lost or stolen.

Some users, however, may decide to manually update the software because they want to look at the updates to decide whether or not to download them. The updates may be considered to be intrusive or not appropriate.

Security software can also be manually updated or scheduled to download updates. This, as with the operating system, can leave the computer system vulnerable to attacks. For example, if the updates are checked at 5p.m. each evening and new viruses are released overnight then the computer system will have no protection against these all through the next working day.

Hints and tips

You must ensure that you know about the different ways in which operating systems and security software can be updated. You should also consider how these methods of updating will affect a business. Exam questions may ask you about these methods of updating operating systems and security software.

Exam-type questions

1 Describe **two** problems that could occur if the dentist manually updates their security software. [4 marks]

2 Describe **one** advantage to the supermarket of automatically updating their operating system software. [2 marks]

Unit 2
Using ICT to create business solutions

Unit 2 Using ICT to create business solutions

Introduction

In this unit you will use a wide range of applications that are commonly used in business. You will learn how to select the most appropriate software to complete tasks to meet specified business requirements in a variety of contexts. You will learn how to use software tools to handle data for a range of business purposes and apply formatting to enhance documents to suit their purpose and intended audience.

When you complete your OCR assessment, you will be given a business scenario and will be asked to complete a number of tasks. This book has been designed to help you to understand how businesses use ICT, and how the purpose and audience influence the software you choose and the type of documents you create.

You will already have developed skills in the software packages you will be using. You should be able to use word processing, desktop publishing (DTP), spreadsheet, database, presentation, web page, graphics and email software. You should also be able to use the internet. This book is not designed to teach you the software skills – if you need to develop these skills there are other resources on the market that will help you do this, such as the OCR Cambridge Nationals in ICT Level 1/2 Dynamic Learning. This book has been designed to help you to gain the knowledge and understanding of how to apply these skills in a business environment. It should help you to decide which software package is the most suitable to use for the tasks you need to complete.

As you work through this unit you will be introduced to six different companies. You will learn how the employees of these companies use IT to produce solutions to solve common business problems. You will learn how to organise your work and increase your efficiency when using IT, and will see how this can be applied when producing solutions to business problems. You will also learn how to design and format documents that are fit for a business purpose.

There is frequently more than one way to produce an IT solution to a business problem. Often there is no right answer, just wrong ones! If the solution makes efficient use of IT, meets the requirements of the task, is suitable for the target audience and is formatted appropriately, then you will have solved the problem. Look at how the employees of the companies in this book solve the problems they are faced with. Can you think of another way the employees could have solved the problem? Would this way have been just as efficient? Would it be suitable for the target audience? Would it meet all the requirements of the task? As you work through this book, you might like to discuss alternative ways of solving the problems, as a class or with your teacher.

Hints and tips have been included, which will help you to focus on what the examiner will be looking for when they are assessing your work.

To prepare yourself for the OCR R002 assessment, you should work through the OCR practice assignments (available from the OCR website). Use this book to see how the employees mentioned have approached similar tasks. Check that, like the employees in this book, you have:

- taken into consideration the purpose and the target audience
- selected the most appropriate software for the task
- selected the most appropriate type of document
- used your ICT skills efficiently
- checked your work and corrected any errors
- formatted your documents appropriately.

Look at the tables that show good and bad design – check that you have included the good points and avoided the bad points. Read the hints and tips and check that you have applied these to your work.

When you are given your OCR assignment, read through the scenario carefully and make sure you understand the nature and purpose of the business, then read through all the tasks so that you have a clear idea of what you will need to do in the time you have been given. Although this might seem like you are wasting time, in reality, this will actually give you a far better idea of what you have to do and will help you to plan your time wisely.

Before you start each task, read it very carefully to make sure you understand what is required. Look back at the scenario to see if there is any information that will help you to decide which software would be most suitable and what type of document would be most suitable for your target audience.

Make sure you attempt all tasks. Even if you find part of a task difficult, do the parts that you can do, and present this as clearly as you can, as you are likely to be given some marks for the parts that you have completed.

When you are working on your assignment, organise your work in a folder structure, making sure you save your work frequently, using suitable file and folder names. Use version control so you can easily see which file is the most recent. Remember to make regular backups of your work.

When you have completed your OCR assignment, check your work carefully to ensure that all documents are formatted appropriately and consistently. Read through each task again and make sure that your solution meets the requirements of the task and is suitable for the target audience. Check that you have used the tools and facilities of your software efficiently. Make sure that you have spellchecked and proofread your work to ensure it is grammatically correct and free from error. If you have a printed solution, make sure that the print layout is appropriate and that all the required data is fully displayed. When you are satisfied that you have completed all the tasks to the best of your ability, hand your completed work in to your teacher.

Good luck!

1

Getting started

Starting your assignment

When you are given your assignment you are, in effect, acting as a designer. The designer's role is to draw up and produce a solution to the given task brief – taking into account any relevant **societal**, **cultural** and audience needs, and safety issues to ensure the product is right. In other words you will need to follow the normal accepted practices of business organisations.

All designers will work first on a *design specification*.

What you need to do ☑

Make sure that you fully understand the task set including:
- what is required?
  - ➤ data requirements
  - ➤ what you need to research
  - ➤ type of documents to be produced
- who is the audience and what is the purpose of the documents you produce?
  - ➤ type of audience, including
    - social economic group
    - gender
    - age
    - education
    - interest, etc.
- the time you can give to completing the task.

Design specification

This is possibly the most important stage of the design process and yet one of the least understood. It is important that before you produce a 'solution' there is a true understanding of the actual user's needs as this will help you to choose the correct methods, documents and software.

The design specification is a document listing what the needs of the task are in detail. The designer should constantly refer back to this document to ensure designs are appropriate. You may find that drawing up such a specification will help you to decide how best to answer your assignment.

There are often key pieces of information in the task itself. Let's examine one of the case study companies. Based upon the following case study text, carefully read and see if you can identify the types of documents and software that might be useful to the company.

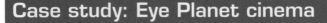

Case study: Eye Planet cinema

Two of the employees at the cinema are Dihana Simons and Jamal Ali.

Let's first examine the case study company and pick out some of the key information needed.

The cinema features four screens with digital and traditional projection systems. The cinema is often used by businesses for corporate presentations and sales meetings. Special children's parties are catered for where popcorn, hot dogs, soft drinks and film ticket packages are discounted. The Eye Planet cinema chain recently won the best catering in a cinema award.

The cinema opens and shows its first films from 2.30p.m. every day and is generally closed by 12.30a.m. in the morning. It serves popcorn (sweet, salted and hot buttered), four flavours of soft drinks, bottled water, ice creams, pre-packed sweets, pick-your-own sweets, nachos and pizza slices. Self-serve dispensers provide tomato sauce and mustard. Soft drinks are also self-service.

The cinema has an automated ticket collection booth for pre-booked tickets. Recently, the operation has added online ticket booking systems, which offer lower-priced tickets for pre-bookings. Concessions are available for children, students, senior citizens and the unemployed. There are five levels of Planeteer membership: Basic Planeteer (any age), Junior Planeteer (5–15), Silver Planeteer (15–18), Gold Planeteer (18+) and Platinum Planeteer (any age).

Four postcard dispensers for advertisers are dotted around the reception and there are two advertising boards for these postcard advertisements next to the ticket sales counter.

Just part of the description above gives us a large amount of information on the types of ICT that will be used and the target audiences.

If we explore the types of audiences:

Concessions are available for children, students, senior citizens and the unemployed. There are five levels of Planeteer membership: Basic Planeteer (any age), Junior Planeteer (5–15), Silver Planeteer (15–18), Gold Planeteer (18+) and Platinum Planeteer (any age).

From this information we can research the audience (user) needs and the most appropriate ways to communicate with them.

Jamal decided to write a short blog article clearly directed at a certain audience – students and young people. He chose to use a blog as this is a useful way to communicate with a younger audience. It is informal and direct. Here's how it begins:

> Time for the summer vacation and we have lots of fun deals for Gold Planeters during the summer break. It's party time all of the time at Eye Planet with free popcorn and cool films that rock until after the midnight hour.

But Jamal chose to use the local newspaper for another piece of writing intended for a very different audience – senior citizens. As you can see Jamal's choice of media and writing style is very different:

> Government-funded grants allow us to offer film classics every Wednesday afternoon at competitive discounted prices for all pensioners.

The two pieces of writing are different but they are both basically trying to impart information to the customer who is the end user. Jamal has chosen different media and different writing styles, and this means he will have to use different software too.

The first example is intended to give students added incentives to visit the cinema and it is informal, chatty and warm, while the second is more informal, factual and business-like.

Type of communication	Writing style	Communication method
Informal	Usually used with friends and family Often contains shortened versions of words Sometimes contains slang words	Blogs, tweets, informal letters, informal emails, newsletters and posters for young informal audiences
Formal	Used in a professional business setting No slang words Uses correct grammar	Presentations, formal letters, business websites, invoices, contracts, legal documents, leaflets, catalogues, etc.

As we can see it is not just writing style that changes according to audience. Businesses must also look at the different types of documents that would be appropriate to communicate with the audience and then select the best software for the task.

In other case studies the audience information is slightly harder to find but we still have clues in the text.

Hints and tips

- Before you rush into your task, take some time to draw up a specification of needs.
- Read carefully through the entire assignment so that you are aware of all the tasks that you need to complete.
- Check that you have all the files that you will need to complete the tasks.
- Open any files you have been given so that you know what they contain.
- Organise your filing structure.

Case study: Cushington Ceramic Seals

> Cushington Ceramic Seals is a large manufacturing company producing ceramic components for *the space and aircraft* industry. Most of the company's products *are sold to other companies* producing equipment for *military use.*

As you can see from the phrases highlighted above this company will use mainly formal communication methods.

You should read the context very carefully and identify the audience before starting your project.

2

Storing electronic data and information

Specification coverage

- File and folder naming:
  - meaningful file and folder names
  - folder structure
- Version control
- Security:
  - backups
  - password protection
  - compressing/zipping files

What you will learn

To understand how to create effective file structures, formats and names for data collected.

Introduction

Let's look at another case study company – the SaverShop supermarket.

Again, carefully read the case study text and see if you can identify the types of documents and software that might be useful to the company.

Case study: SaverShop supermarket

Two of the staff that work at the SaverShop supermarket are Naomi Johnson and Ira Huda.

SaverShop has been in the town since 1982. They offer competitively branded products with lots of variety, as well as their own less expensive ranges.

SaverShop has been a firmly established community food retailer for over 125 years and is recognised for its excellent fresh food, friendly staff and value for money.

The SaverShop supermarket chain operates over 212 stores and employs in excess of 3000 staff.

In order to help keep ahead in the fiercely competitive retail industry, the past few years have seen the successful development of niche concepts to meet the varying lifestyles, locations and shopping needs of the customer.

The store also supplies specialist products, computer games at budget prices, cheap TVs, DVDs and some jeans and trainers in their mission to offer value to their customers.

Opening hours are from 8a.m. to 11p.m. six days a week. The store offers a special shopper and delivery service for disabled shoppers in the local area, free of charge.

Ira Huda who works at SaverShop needed to create a file structure to store electronic data files on new products.

- Before she could start creating any documents, she needed to understand how to store them on the supermarket's computer system so that she could easily find them again. Ira knew that setting up a good electronic filing system would save her a lot of time in the future. All companies need to have a good system for organising files. This is because they often have more than one user of what is produced. This is called file management. With over 3000 employees and a large number of documents a well-organised filing system is vital.

File management

What is file management?

File management is organising and keeping track of files and folders. It is also related to file naming.

> ### What you need to do ☑️
>
> Make sure that you carefully organise your files.
> - Use sensible filenames:
>   - ➤ Choose names that you and other people will understand.
>   - ➤ Include a date or version number.
> - Set up sensibly named folders and sub-folders:
>   - ➤ Remember it's not just you who needs to understand the names of the folders.
>   - ➤ Add sub-folders, again using sensible names.
> - Always backup your data.

Why is file management important?

It helps Ira to stay organised, so that information can be easily located either by her or by other *authorised* people working at the supermarket. Setting up a good structure with a sensible file name saves time in the long term.

A sensible file name is a name that describes the information that is contained in the file. Ira calls her file 'New_Milk_Products_23April2012_V01'.

What does naming convention mean?

This is all about giving appropriate file names to the files created. For example, another document Ira created is called 'New_Products_Research_v01_12Sept2012.doc'. As she edited the document she saved it as 'New_Products_Research_v02_14Sept2012.doc', etc. where v01 represents Version 1. Ira also added a date so that she could see when she last updated the file without even opening it.

Having named the file sensibly, Ira needed to create a folder structure to store the documents.

Folders, sub-folders and files – what's the difference?

Folders

A folder is a container for storing files. You could think of this as similar to a drawer in your bedroom cupboard, where each drawer only contains related documents. You could make the drawer a blue clothes drawer or a socks drawer.

Sub-folders

A sub-folder is a folder within a folder (a little like having a box in the drawer). For example, you might have a folder named as your own name and then within that you might want separate folders for your homework, and your personal documents. Within the homework folder you might want a folder for each subject and within the personal folder you might want to divide it into different categories. The folder structure would look something like this:

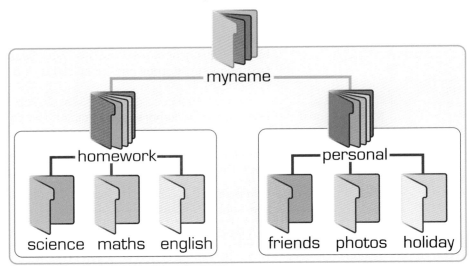

Files

Ira knows that the names she uses for the folders must be understandable to others. She can't call a folder or file by her own name or they will not know what it is.

A file is the name given to every document that you save on your computer, whether it is a word-processed document, a spreadsheet, database, an image or a presentation.

Different software produces files of different file types. Sometimes these can be identified by their file extension. Some of these file types do not retain the formatting of data, etc. When Ira saves her files she must save them using her software's normal file type (and/or as a PDF) so that the formatting and features she has used are not lost!

Some of the most common file types Ira uses are shown below:

Text files		What the format means
.doc and .docx	Microsoft Word document	Saves as a Word document complete with formatting but can usually only be opened using the same or a later version of Microsoft Word.
.msg	Microsoft Outlook mail message	Saves as an Outlook mail document complete with formatting but can usually only be opened using the same or a later version of Microsoft Outlook.
.rtf	Rich text format file	Saves as a rich text file complete with formatting for the text. Can be opened in almost any word processor.
.txt	Plain text file	Saves as a text file without formatting – only the words are kept. Any formatting, graphics, etc. will be lost. Can be opened by most software.
Data files		
.csv	Comma separated values file	Saves as a text file complete with commas to separate data.
.ppt and .pptx	PowerPoint presentation	Saves as a PowerPoint slideshow pps/ppsx file that can run as a self running show.
.xml	XML file	XML files have become a standard way of storing and transferring data between programs over the internet. Because they are formatted as text documents, they can be edited by a basic text editor.
Audio files		
.m4a	MPEG-4 audio file	Used to store compressed audio and video data by people such as iTunes.
.mid	MIDI file	Standard MIDI (musical instrument digital interface) file used in music authoring and mixing programs.
.mp3	MP3 audio file	Compressed audio format used by most portable music players, such as the Apple iPod and Microsoft Zune.
.wav	WAVE audio file	WAV music files are most often seen on Windows-based computers.
.wma	Windows Media audio file	Audio file compressed with Windows Media – a format developed by Microsoft.
Video files		
.avi	Audio Video Interleave file	Video format created by Microsoft.
.flv	Flash video file	Animation or video file usually created in Adobe Flash.
.mov	Apple QuickTime Movie	A movie file created in QuickTime.
Image files		
.bmp	Bitmap image file	Uncompressed image file built up using a rectangular grid of pixels. Produced using paint programs.
.jpg	JPEG Image	Used for storing digital photos.
.pdf	Portable Document Format file	Cross-platform document used for email attachments or for saving publications in a standard format for viewing on different computers. PDF files may contain text, images and other data.

Hints and tips

Like Ira you must produce a well-structured, logical system to store your electronic information.

- *All* your folders must have meaningful names.
- *All* your files must be saved in an appropriate file type with meaningful names and, where appropriate, versions of file(s) must be clearly identified.
- *All* files must be stored logically within the folder structure.
- Remember that in a business, files are used by other people so the file names must mean something to the business not just to the user.

Case study: Ben's Dental Surgery

Two of the staff members at the dental surgery are Ben Clark and Lucy Bhat.

The surgery's opening hours are 9a.m. to 6p.m., Monday to Friday. Its emergency contact number is 03791 756254.

The surgery specialises in and has a superb reputation for caring for nervous patients. Five dentists work at the surgery.

The range of normal services available includes routine examinations, orthodontic care, white, silver (normal) and gold fillings, crowns, bleaching, precision dentures, mouth guards and referrals. Safety and cross-infection prevention are of paramount importance to the practice in order to safeguard both staff and patients against blood-borne infections.

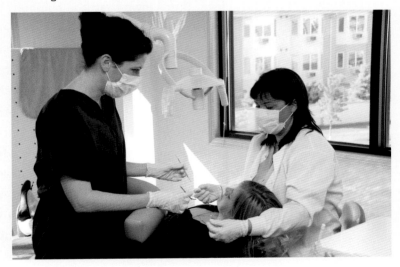

The surgery has toilet facilities, a local advertisement board (which is free to all) and TVs in the waiting and surgery rooms.

A retail counter in the reception makes available a wide range of dental and dental hygiene products. Bookings are done on computer.

The dental surgery buys products in the UK and Europe so often has to convert currency between pounds and euros.

Lucy works at Ben's Dental Surgery as a receptionist. She had carefully created a record of bookings but the file had accidentally been over-written by a temporary receptionist whilst she was on holiday. Fortunately Lucy had made a backup on her flash drive.

Computer data can easily get lost or destroyed. Lucy always protects her data by making a backup of her files. Backup means saving a copy of a file, or a group of files, and storing them in a different place away from the computer. Lucy makes a backup on a portable disk or storage device – usually on her memory stick. Backups can also be made to another computer on the same network, or even to a server on the internet. The key thing is that you keep the backup away from the site where the original file is. This provides protection against physical loss from fire or theft.

Lucy knows that she will need a backup copy of her files to either restore the whole folder if there is a system failure or to restore a document when the **Undo** command merely isn't enough to fix a mistake.

She sometimes thinks that a backup copy of all the files seems to be a wasted use of storage space and time, but also knows that she must consider the time that she might save by avoiding data loss. She knows that it is company policy to create backups on a regular basis when there are several users updating company files such as the database. Without a backup copy, she could not restore corrupted or missing data or any incorrect changes to the database.

Lucy has to consider how often she should backup the files.

This generally depends on how often the documents and data have major changes made to them. She knows that there are some general guidelines to help her decide on the frequency of backups:

- If the data is used only for reference and rarely changed, it is sufficient to create backups only when the data is changed.
- If the data is active and the data frequently changes, she must create a schedule to regularly backup the files.
- If the data has multiple users, as with the company database, she must create a backup copy of the data whenever there is a change.

Key word

Undo

- Make sure that you fully understand the size and type of files you use.
- Use a file type that will keep the 'features' you have used in producing your solution – for example, the formulae in a spreadsheet, or the format and imported graphics, etc. in a document.
- Backup your files to an external drive.
- Change the resolution of images, etc. to suit their use.
- Zip large files when sending them via email.
- Where you need to email a number of files, group them together in a folder and zip the folder.

Backups

Let's take another look at this company – Ben's Dental Surgery – and its policy on storing data and information.

Zipped files

Some of the files Lucy produces are very large. To save on space she zips them.

Lucy knows that zipping a file creates a compressed version of the file that is considerably smaller than the original file. The zipped version of Lucy's file would then have a .zip file extension. Lucy zipped a Microsoft Office Word document called Dental-List_V01.doc that was 6.5 megabytes (MB) in size. Dental-List_V01.zip, reduced its size to just over a megabyte.

The file types that are reduced in size the most as a result of zipping are text files (such as .txt, .docx, .xls) and graphics files that use non-compressed file types such as .bmp. Some graphics files, such as .jpg and .gif, already use compression; therefore the file size is reduced very little by zipping. Also, a Word document that is full of graphics files does not get reduced as much as a document that is mostly text. Lucy often zips the whole folder containing a number of files for archive/sharing purposes.

Some advantages of zipping a file or folder are:

- Lucy saves storage space. Zipping large files can save up to 80% or more in hard disk space.
- Smaller file sizes drastically reduce email transmission time.
- The email messages and attachments take up less space, which is useful when her mailbox has a space limit.
- Many zip utilities allow her to encrypt files and protect sensitive data, especially when she sends it attached to an email.
- She can send and receive email attachments, such as .exe files, that would otherwise be blocked by email software for security reasons.
- It is courteous to the recipient of the email because it saves space in their mailbox.
- There is less chance of an email being rejected by the server on the basis of size.
- It enables downloading of a single zipped folder rather than having to download several attached files individually.

Attaching multiple files to an email

Lucy often has to attach a large number of files to an email. Sometimes she will put the files into a folder and then zip the folder to create a single file to add to the email as this is much simpler for her than attaching lots of separate files.

Password protecting documents

Most of Lucy's files are confidential. As she shares a computer with someone else it is possible for others to gain access to her hard drive. Because of this she adds password protection to some of her documents that contain sensitive information.

Lucy also often uses a password to prevent modification – this allows anyone to open the document to read it, but they would not be able to change it in any way. As with any password, the one Lucy chooses for her documents are easy for her to remember, but difficult for others to guess. She is careful to avoid common passwords such as 'password', birthdates, pet names, astrological signs, etc. Lucy knows that letter–number combinations tend to work best with a number of both upper and lower case letters.

Lucy also knows that passwords are not fail-safe. There are web services that will hack into files for you. While this is comforting should she forget her password, it means that others may also be able to access her protected files.

3

Searching for data and information: research skills

▶ What you will learn

To understand how to effectively search for data and information, checking its accuracy and relevance.

Introduction

Let's go back to an earlier case study company – Eye Planet cinema. Dihana Simons, who works at the cinema, was asked to search for the most popular films from the last five years.

The trouble is it's a jungle out there – a 'jungle of information' that is. There is so much information on films to access these days that it is difficult for Dihana to sift through and sort everything to find exactly what she is looking for in order to satisfy her research needs.

Doing research is a bit like going on an adventure and heading into 'unknown territory'. When you are exploring a new topic, you don't know exactly what you will find on the journey. But Dihana knew that with the right research methods she would have a greater chance of getting to where she needed to go.

With research she could simply switch on the computer and surf the internet for hours until she hopefully came across what she was looking for, or she could take the time to identify her information needs. As time was short and she was being employed to do the research, the second option was the best for her.

Dihana had a number of ways that she could find the information, but first she knew that she had to follow a research method that would prove effective:

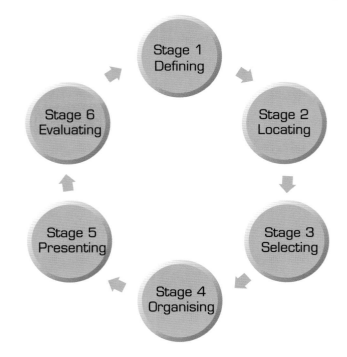

Stage 1 – Defining her task and posing her research questions.

Stage 2 – Locating the resources/information she needs to complete the task.

Stage 3 – Selecting the relevant information to answer her research question(s).

Stage 4 – Organising and synthesising the information into a logical and easy to understand outcome that reflects her original task.

Stage 5 – Presenting her finished outcome to her boss.

Stage 6 – Evaluating her research and presentation for future tasks – what worked well and what could be improved.

Defining the task

When you are on a journey you always need to do some pre-planning to work out what it is that you are hoping to achieve. What will be the outcome or purpose of the journey? Doing research is no different.

You can start by asking the following questions:

1 Why am I doing this task?

2 What do I want to produce at the end of the task?

3 What do I really want to find out?

4 What am I going to be assessed on?

5 What difference will this research make?

6 What is the time frame in which I must complete this task?

Focus questions

There is a saying, 'The question is the answer' and if you think about it, that is true. The kind of questions you ask will determine the type of information you will collect. So the more considered your questions the better chance you will find relevant information that shows a deep understanding of your topic.

Case study: Leisure centre

Two of the members of staff working at a leisure centre are Ria Mathews and Kieran Allan.

The centre is situated in East Road and offers a wide range of activities and facilities suitable for everyone.

Opening hours:

Monday	7a.m. to 10p.m.
Tuesday	6a.m. to 10p.m.
Wednesday	7a.m. to 10p.m.

Thursday	6a.m. to 10p.m.
Friday	7a.m. to 10p.m.
Saturday	8a.m. to 10p.m.
Sunday	8a.m. to 10p.m.

The sports hall boasts the ability to stage almost any sport. Visitors can participate in some of the many clubs including abseiling, canoeing and aikido.

Many people participate in weight training and improve their fitness by using the superb gym with all the latest equipment and expert tuition. There is also a 25m swimming pool (the big pool), a dive pool/pit, a learner pool and a water slide for the adventurous. The leisure centre also hosts a junior tennis tournament. All local schools are invited to take part and coaching sessions are offered in the four weeks leading up to the competition. There is also *The Messenger*'s annual sponsored swim.

Adults can relax in the luxurious health suite, which includes sauna, steam room, jacuzzi and solarium.

The leisure centre runs special play schemes every weekend and all through the school holidays, for children of all ages. The latest addition to the centre is a supervised skatepark.

At certain points in term time local schools have priority and exclusive access to the facilities. The sports hall at the centre is large enough to host most sports and includes a special arena seating system that can accommodate up to 600 spectators, as well as facilitating the full size pitches and courts for a full range of sports.

The 25m swimming pool, dive pool, learner pool and water slide are available to private clubs, schools and the general public.

The centre actively welcomes customers with disabilities and offers dedicated parking, induction loops, designated changing and toilet facilities, pool hoist, lifts as appropriate, automatic entrance doors and discounted rates on certain activities.

Kieran works at the leisure centre. At first sight you may think that the leisure centre has similar needs to the Eye Planet cinema but the audience is actually quite different. The majority of visitors are interested in sport and healthy living. Keiran has been asked to research the possibility of opening a healthy food cafe for teenagers.

Keiran believes that things that make teenagers choose different types of food include how hungry they are, food cravings, the appeal of food, how much time they have to eat, convenience of the food,

food availability, parental influence on eating behaviours (including the culture or religion of the family), benefits of foods (including health), mood, body image, habit, cost, media and vegetarian principles.

But his colleague at the centre, Ria, believes that the major barriers to eating more fruits, vegetables and healthy products, and eating fewer high-fat foods include a lack of sense of urgency about personal health. Teenagers are still young and they have other things that are more important to them, and they prefer the taste of other more unhealthy foods.

Her suggestions for helping teenagers eat a more healthy diet include making healthy foods taste and look better, limiting the availability of unhealthy options in the cafe, making healthy food more available and convenient, teaching teenagers good eating habits at an early age and changing social norms to make it 'cool' to eat healthily.

Let's explore another business use of searching techniques.

Secondary research

Kieran starts with **secondary research**. This is about using data that already exists. It involves collecting and summarising existing research. There are a range of resources available for secondary research. The most well known are:

- published statistics
- published texts
- media
- personal documents.

Advantages and disadvantages of **secondary** research

Advantages	Disadvantages
• Cheap and accessible – especially in a library and on the internet • Often the only resource, for example historical documents • Only way to examine large-scale trends	• Lack of consistency of perspective • Biases and inaccuracies can't always be checked • Published statistics often raise more questions than they answer • The concern over whether *any* data can be totally separated from why it was collected in the first place

The accuracy of secondary source information is very important. Keiran needs to carefully review the electronic information found.

What you need to do ☑

Plan before you start your research:

- Explore the research needs for your task:
  - ➤ What are the key words?
  - ➤ What are the key phrases you will use?
- Explore the advanced search functions for your chosen search engine.
- Decide how you will record your findings.

Reviewing sources of information

Source	Review techniques
e-books and CD-ROMS	Most e-books and CD-ROMS are initially reviewed by publishers or editors for quality of content and writing style, as well as marketability. When evaluating an e-book or CD-ROM, you should check these basic points: ● Author or contact person – brief biographical information may also be included ● Publisher ● Date of publication ● Intended audience – determined by examining the content, preface and introduction ● Purpose of the information – determined by examining the content, preface and introduction.
Online magazines and newspapers	Online newspapers and popular or general interest magazines and blogs usually have staff writers who are responsible for writing in certain areas. Scholarly journal articles generally undergo a more rigorous peer-review process. Experts in the subject field review the article manuscript before publication to ensure reliability and credibility. When evaluating a periodical publication, you should check these basic points: ● Author or contact person ● Editorial board – members, with their affiliations, may be listed ● Publisher ● Date of publication ● Intended audience – determined by examining the content; publication may state intended audience in note on contents page ● Purpose of the information – determined by examining the content.
Internet search engines	Information on the internet, unless it is from one of the areas above, is mostly unfiltered, requiring extra caution in selecting reliable sources. Virtually anyone can create a website on a topic, regardless of their training, education or experience in the subject field. You may also find email messages and newsgroup postings in your search results, as well as business-related or commercial sites, posted by companies whose primary purpose is to convince consumers of the value of their products or services. When evaluating a website, you should check these basic points: ● Author or contact person – usually located in the footer ● Information held on other websites ● Link to local home page – usually located in either header or footer ● Institution – usually located in either header or footer ● Domain – the last segment of the 'root' of the URL ● Date of creation or revision – usually located in footer ● Intended audience – determined by examining the content ● Purpose of the information – determined by examining the content.

There are many ways in which Kieran could research the particular information that he wants to find out about – he could use online newspapers, books, images, maps, DVDs and CDs. There are advantages and disadvantages to using each of these sources. Kieran decided to use the internet for all of his research.

Much of the research we do today is done on the internet so let's look at how to search the internet effectively. Kieran used a web browser to conduct his research.

What is a browser?

A browser is a gateway to the internet. It makes the internet easy and manageable to use. Some of the most popular browsers are Internet Explorer, Safari, Opera and Firefox.

What is a search engine?

Web-based *search engines* are programs that search for sites on the internet based on the '*criteria*' you have asked for. The suggested sites that are returned are called *results*. Two of the most popular search engines are Google and Yahoo but there are many more and as they often return different results, you will need to explore the advanced search options for your chosen search engine so that you can use the search engine effectively.

What are 'search criteria'?

This is the selection of words that you type into the search box in the search engine.

Search engines are very different from the indexes you find in a book and are called directories on the internet. People can catalogue pages in a subject directory, but search engines rely on computer programs called spiders to search the web and log the words on each page, as they have to process thousands of new pages added to the web each day. It would not be possible for people to do this, but because the system is automated, choosing the best search criteria is vitally important.

The techniques used for searching in a search engine are similar to those used in any database.

With a search engine, Kieran needs to type his keywords related to his healthy eating topic into a search 'box'.

The search engine will then scan its database and return a web page with links to websites containing the word or words he specified.

Because these databases are very large, most search engines will return many thousands of results.

Without search strategies or techniques, finding what he needs will be impossible. Kieran must understand how his particular search engine works.

To use search engines effectively, it is essential that Kieran applies techniques that will narrow results and show the most relevant pages at the top of the results list.

To do this he uses the following search strategies.

He could use a Boolean search with some search engines but some do not support this.

Phrase searching

Kieran knows how to use phrase searching.

Surrounding a group of words with double quotes tells the search engine to only find documents in which those words appear side by side.

Kieran knows that phrase searching is a powerful search technique for significantly narrowing his search results within his chosen search engine. His phrase search would look like this:

> **"Healthy eating"**

Kieran knows that some search engines interpret lower case letters as either upper or lower case but others need the correct capitals.

Domain search

Sometimes Kieran uses a domain search.

Kieran can do a domain search because he understands the term URL. A URL (uniform resource locator) is the unique address for a file that is accessible on the internet. A common way to get to a website is to enter the URL of its home page file in the web browser's address line.

What you need to do ✓

Make sure that you fully understand how to refine your research:

- What search engines will you use?
  - ➤ How can you use them to narrow down a search?
- What other online searches will you do?
  - ➤ Online databases.
  - ➤ Online dictionaries.
- How can you refine your searches?
  - ➤ Use of search within results options?
  - ➤ Advanced search options?
- How will you record your sources of information?

Domains sometimes have country codes in their URL such as .co.uk. You can only have a .co.uk domain if you are based in the UK. Kieran wants data from this type of domain. This is because he does not really want data from around the world. He is only interested in data from the UK.

He knows that .co.uk will give him only UK based data, so he adds this to his search criteria.

How can you refine your search to get better results?

Kieran uses quotation marks in his search engine to find a specific phrase, for example "healthy eating". He knows that this phrase will bring back thousands of hits, whereas without the quotation marks it will return close to 38 million pages. By selecting the pages from the UK only button in his search engine he finds 111,000 hits when he uses quotation marks, which is still too many for him to look through.

Kieran's chosen search engine has other useful features such as a 'Search within results' option. He decides to make use of this and narrows down the number of pages.

Sometimes Kieran doesn't know what *exactly* he is looking for. That's when wild-card searches come in handy. A wild-card search can be used as a placeholder for any sequence of characters or words. These wild-card characters include *, # and ?, with the asterisk being the most common.

Many search engines let you substitute asterisks for single letters within search phrases, so Kieran could search for 'health*' and find 'healthy'. Kieran is using Google and he knows that it does not allow this type of search on single words. However, Google automatically does something very similar each time Kieran searches as it uses what is called stemming technology to find variations of each word in his search. For example, searching for 'diet' automatically finds variations such as 'dietary' and 'diets'.

Most search engines will find a missing word in a phrase. Kieran simply has to substitute an asterisk. For example, 'Coca-Cola was invented by *'. Kieran can also search for phrases with or without quotation marks, but he knows that using the quotation marks is often more effective than leaving them off. Quotation marks force Google to find the exact phrase within the quotes, except for the wild-card word.

Kieran also uses wild-card words to help him complete the phrase when he knows almost all the words.

Sometimes Kieran uses a number of asterisks in a search phrase.

Advanced search pages

Another possibility for Kieran is to use an advanced search page. Not all search engines have these, but most do. The one shown below is the one Kieran uses in Google.

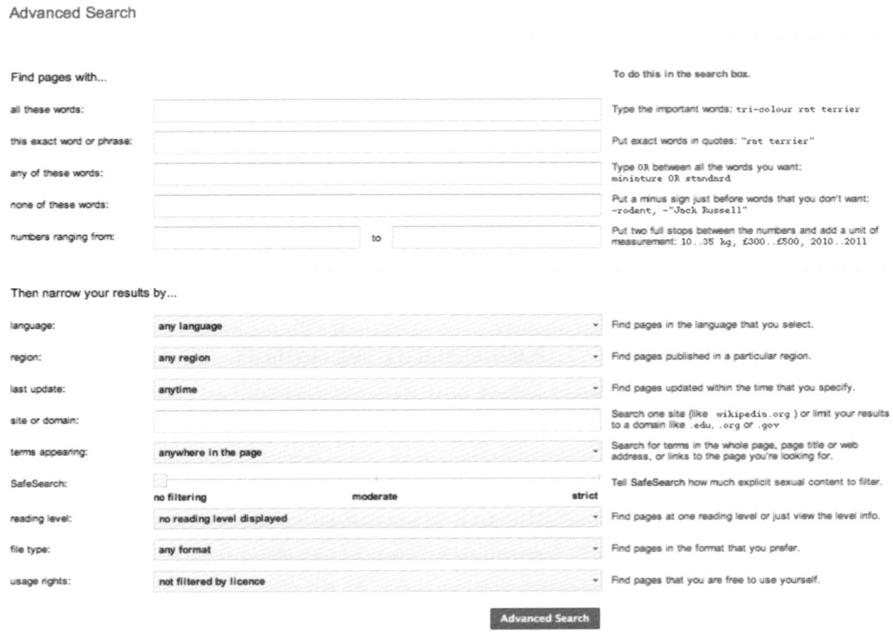

Copyright

Kieran knew that when preparing a document, he must always keep a list of all the websites he uses as references because he would need to acknowledge his sources later on. He knows that he must *never* copy or use someone else's work without crediting them.

There is a law about copying information, called copyright, and it's a law he has to abide by. The copyright symbol © means he needs to get permission to copy the information if he wants to use it for his company. Even if he just wants to use it for his own purpose, he must record the source, for example the name of the website. Much of the data on the web is copyright even if it does not have this symbol.

Search engines such as Google do not own the copyright of content; other people do, the people who wrote the content. You must find out who they are if you plan to use content from the web.

Normally a published work on the internet will include a copyright notice giving details of the copyright holder(s). Where there is no copyright notice, if there are publisher or author details you should contact the author or publisher and check the copyright in the work. If you cannot trace the publisher, or if they have gone out of business, then you will have to trace the author or any descendants of the author if they are dead.

Make sure that you fully understand copyright:

- Do not breach copyright laws:
  - ➤ Check the copyright information of anything you want to use
  - ➤ Ask for permission to use the content if it is copyrighted
  - ➤ Re-write content in your own words
  - ➤ Try to use copyright free images and if these have terms and conditions attached – ensure you know what these are and that you comply with them.
- Acknowledge the sources of information and remember content is not owned by the search engine.

If you take an image or any other content from the internet and it has been created by somebody else, then copyright law protects the owner from having their work used or changed illegally. It protects all sorts of information such as photographs, music, video, broadcasts, text and sound recordings.

Accuracy of information and data

Kieran found over 40,000 websites that included information that he was searching for, so how should he decide which ones to believe?

Think about it!

Just because you see it online, doesn't mean it's true. How can you tell a reliable website from an unreliable site?

Evaluating websites

Is information on websites reliable, accurate and up to date? How do you know which sources you can trust? How do you know whether the site is giving you facts or opinion? What's biased? – how can you tell. Is the information relevant to your needs?

Source – where does the information come from?

Knowing where information comes from can help you decide how good it is. Information found on the internet is likely to be more reliable if it comes from a government, academic or not-for-profit website rather than a blog or personal website.

Fact, opinion and bias

When conducting research Keiran has to be aware of bias. Bias is when you judge something based on a distorted view, not how it actually is. For example, a company may think that its products are the best even if there are better options. Other biased views can be due to political, religious or stereotype views, which can be based upon an individual's experience, background or even gender.

You need to be aware that information that tries to sell products or make people either vote a certain way or believe in something will be biased – favouring one thing over another. This does not mean that the information has no value but it may be necessary to look at information from several sources to get a wider view.

Does the information relate to your needs?

When searching on the internet, make sure that the search words you use accurately describe what you are looking for. Search engines find the most relevant pages first, based on what you have asked for.

You will usually be able to find a date on most reliable websites, for example all the news sites have dates of updates. For some information it is important that the information is up to date, for example when researching the cost of a product, but for other information (for example, to find an image of the Houses of Parliament) the date it was created is not really relevant.

To help him find the information again, Kieran saved any useful websites he found in his favourites or bookmarked them. Bookmarks and favourites are essentially the same thing and the terminology used depends on the browser.

Hints and tips

You must use effective search criteria when looking for information. Use carefully chosen criteria in a search engine to find appropriate information, which fully meets the specified requirements. Remember to record the copyright holder(s) of the information found accurately and thoroughly. You must also create folders and organise your bookmarks.

Organising bookmarks and favourites

Bookmarks (called 'Favorites' in Internet Explorer) record an internet URL so you can revisit it later without having to remember its address.

Keeping bookmarks enables Kieran to easily revisit the sites he likes without having to remember their exact URLs.

Using bookmarks he can collect lists of good sites, and build up a library of his favourite and most useful websites.

Once he has added a bookmark to his list, he simply selects it from his browser's bookmark list to revisit the page.

He adds a page to his bookmarks by visiting it and using his browser's add bookmark feature.

Internet Explorer

In Internet Explorer go to Favorites/Add to Favorites.

Firefox

Pick up the URL from the address bar with the mouse (double click on address and hold button down) and drag it to the Bookmarks menu at the top of the window, then drag it to the folder you wish from the resulting drop-down list.

Kieran bookmarked a lot of sites so his list was very long. To help him to find the websites he wanted he created a set of bookmark folders.

He managed his list by deciding on a set of category groups choosing sensible names that clearly describe the content in which to store his bookmarks.

Most browsers come with a built-in set of categories and bookmarks, but Keiran created his own so they were not cluttered by sites he does not use.

A representative set of top-level category folders is listed below, with the most frequently used items shown at the top above a separator bar:

```
Healthy eating

Foods

Suppliers

----------

Local

National

Costs
```

Bookmark category management

The three basic skills of bookmark category management Keiran used are described below:

Creation

He created a set of categories for his major interests.

Internet Explorer

Favorites/Organize Favorites/Create Folder

Firefox

Bookmarks/Bookmark Manager/New Folder

Order

He moved the categories of his frequently used sites to the beginning, and arranged the rest in alphabetical order.

Internet Explorer

Favorites/Organize Favorites

– drag items up and down

Firefox

Bookmarks/Manage Bookmarks

– Drag items up and down in right half of window.

Sub-folders

He added sub-folders for subcategories when necessary.

Kieran has bookmarked a number of websites that provide copyright free images which means he can use them without permission.

What you need to do ☑

- Carefully organise your bookmarks/favourites.
- Make sure that you fully record all of your research.
- Bookmark all the pages you find.
- Organise the bookmarks in folders and sub-folders.
- Check the accuracy of the data and information that you find:
  - ➤ Who wrote it?
  - ➤ Date it was produced.
  - ➤ Reliability of source.

4

Sense of audience

Introduction

Case study: Eye Planet cinema

Jamal Ali at the Eye Planet cinema knows the type of people who regularly visit the cinema. Some customers visit twice a week, some less often. Understanding the audience is very important; it helps Jamal to target the right publicity and get more customers.

The Eye Planet cinema publicity is very effective because Jamal knows the readers':

- interest and knowledge
- education, age and gender
- existing ideas and opinions.

He explores the different types of things that would entice them into coming to the cinema. He needs to know that different factors affect people's decisions including their age (especially) and their education. He knows that different subjects excite different people.

All businesses need to understand the:

- purpose of the communication
- needs of the organisation
- audience
- best methods of communication.

To grow a wider audience for the cinema Jamal has to also convince a large number of people who will want to visit different types of films – he actually has a number of different audiences.

He also has a wide range of different types of communication to consider. Sometimes he needs to communicate with lots of people at the same time but at other times he only wants to write to one person.

But it is not just Jamal who needs to use business communications. Let's explore a different company and their needs.

Case study: You Buy estate agent

Two of the members of staff working at the estate agent are Jane Morrison and Azim Ahame.

You Buy is a small independent estate agent selling private properties in the local area, and with a large commercial property department handling 90% of the commercial property in the area.

You Buy have a wide range of customers and potential customers:

- Individuals often rent, buy and sell their houses. You Buy help with every step of the process.
- Businesses need office, factory and shop premises. Some businesses own their own property and others rent them. You Buy helps them to buy, rent and sell business properties including shops, factories and offices.
- Charities own and rent properties. A large number of You Buy's properties for rent are owned by large charities.

The company has done well over the years, representing the builders of various new housing estates, selling the new properties and then reselling the houses as people move on. With a lot of the population commuting to neighbouring Cushington there is a thriving market in the agency's property rental and lettings division.

Opening hours are 9a.m. to 7p.m. six days a week.

The business offers additional services including conveyancing and financial advice, mortgage brokering and household insurance brokering.

You Buy keeps detailed records of both customers and potential customers. They also keep track of the other businesses working in their area very closely.

Being an estate agent, they handle large amounts of money and accurate accounting is very important.

Azim at the You Buy estate agent has a number of very different audiences to Jamal at the cinema. Most of Azim's audience are professional people and his communication methods will be more formal.

What you need to do ☑

Before you choose the best documents to use:
- Identify the end user needs – who are your audience?
  - ➤ Target audience.
- What is the best way to communicate with your audience?
  - ➤ Web or paper based.
- Remember that you are demonstrating business not personal use of ICT:
  - ➤ House style and layout are very important.
- Always check your documents carefully to ensure that there are no errors in them:
  - ➤ Spelling
  - ➤ Grammar
  - ➤ Punctuation
  - ➤ Accuracy.

First let's look at the people Azim at the You Buy estate agent may wish to communicate with:
- Customers and potential customers:
  - ➤ Individuals
  - ➤ Companies
  - ➤ Charities
- Sellers and potential sellers:
  - ➤ Individuals
  - ➤ Companies
  - ➤ Charities
- Lawyers
- Business associates and work colleagues
- Clients, customers and sellers
- Council members.

Unlike Jamal at the cinema who deals mainly with a younger audience who respond to bright colours and modern designs, Azim will be dealing only with adults who buy and rent properties. They will largely be well-educated people who will expect a professional and confidential service. Some of his audience are lawyers and business

owners. He will have to be very careful about what he says and how he presents himself and his company. Azim will need to use both web and paper-based documents, including formal, often legally binding, letters. Accuracy, use of language, spelling and grammar will all be very important.

Now let's consider the most suitable methods of communication.

Communication requirements	Communication methods	Types of software
One to one	Email, letter, phone call or a personal visit	Web browser, email, word processing
One to many	Broadcasts, posters, leaflets, mail-merged letters, presentations, standard web page (for information that doesn't change much), blog or newsgroup (for changing information that needs frequent updating or distribution)	Web design, DTP, word processing, database for mail merge, graphic design, presentation
Many to one	Surveys, web surveys, web forms	Web design, word processing to design questionnaires
One to few	Blog or social networking site (e.g. Facebook)	Web browser
Many to many	Mailing list or newsgroup	Web browser

In selecting the type of documents and the nature of the images and text to use, Azim knows that he must understand his audience and their expectations.

Different types of audience are shown in the following table.

Document	Target audience	What is its purpose?
Go Green T-shirt with 'Save the Trees' slogan	5–30	Promote awareness of environmental sustainability
Leaflet on energy-saving hints and tips	Homeowners/tenants	Help people cut their fuel costs and save the environment
Newsletter of houses on the market	Home buyers	Show potential buyers what is available at the moment
Pamphlet showing jaundiced girl wired up to drip with words 'Three weeks to alcoholic liver shutdown'	Teenagers	Discourage underage/excessive drinking
Poster of people with bad/discoloured teeth from smoking	Teenagers	Promote healthy lifestyles
Poster with cartoon fruit	Young children aged 4–9	Promote healthy eating

Once Azim knows the purpose of his communication and who the audience is, he can choose the best method of communication to use. He can then decide the best software to use for the task.

Different types of software have different uses and often data has to be integrated or transferred from one type of software to another to be modified. Jamal often changes the resolution of an image in graphics software before pasting it into word processing software as he knows the image will be too large causing problems with the file size of the document he is producing.

What you need to do ☑

Think very carefully about your target audience:

- What are the most appropriate communication methods for your task?
  - ➤ Look at similar companies and what they use.
- What types of images should you use?
  - ➤ Research similar companies and see what they use.
- What is the right type of language to use?
  - ➤ Explore the audience's needs carefully including:
    - Language levels
    - Socio-economic group needs.
- Always check your documents carefully to ensure that there are no errors in them:
  - ➤ Spelling
  - ➤ Grammar
  - ➤ Punctuation
  - ➤ Accuracy.

Hints and tips

Remember that whatever type of business document you produce, it must include content that fully meets the specified requirements and is wholly suitable for the target audience. To do this you must first define who the audience is.

5

Types of business documents

▶ *What you will learn*

To understand how to choose the correct type of business document for the needs of a company and its audience.

Introduction

As we saw in the last chapter, Azim Ahame works at the You Buy estate agents. He uses a wide range of business software to communicate with house buyers and sellers. Azim helps with conveyancing (buying and selling houses by transferring important documents) and financial advice (arranging mortgages and household insurance). He has to write to customers in a professional way. The name for this is formal communication.

The purpose of a communication often determines the media used, which then determines the software needed. Of course Azim still has some choices. For example, sometimes spreadsheet software can be used as a database; printed text and graphics could be created in DTP or word-processing software.

Examples of publication	Purpose
Posters Flyers	To attract attention
Leaflets Websites Information points	To provide information to the general public
Presentations Letters Reports Newsletters	To provide information to individuals or groups

If Azim selects the correct software he can start with blank documents and easily choose an appropriate layout and techniques to import, create and edit content. This will apply to his use of all documents including spreadsheets and databases as all business follow a house style. A house style is basically a simple document outlining a design which an organisation will use to make all of its documents look similar.

What you need to do ☑

Remember that you must choose the best types of publication to suit the needs of the task:
- What is required?
- Who is the audience?
- What are the data requirements?
- Which type of publication best suits the needs of the business task?

You must also work out a house style for the company, to include:
- overall design
- use and position of images
- font and size of text
- colours to be used
- position of company logo and address.

You can then select the best type of software for the task:
- Can the task be achieved using one type of software or does it need more than one type of software?

Formal business letters

Azim needs to write formal letters to customers and to the local council. A formal letter is a form of correspondence from an organisation to an external client.

You Buy Estate Agents
Cushington
West Yorkshire
United Kingdom
YO52 3BR

12 July 2012

Mr G Sanderson
Connoll Street
Hill Town
United Kingdom
PR58 5BX

Dear Mr Sanderson

REQUEST FOR RENTAL TERMS – CUSHINGTON BUSINESS PARK

Further to your enquiry about the rental terms of the business unit situated at ref A29 on the Cushington Business Park, the minimum rental period would be two years and the rental cost would be £2500 per calendar month with a £5000 deposit.

I trust this information will satisfy your client's request.

Yours sincerely

Azim Ahame

Azim Ahame

Business Rental Partner
You Buy Estate Agents

Letters:

- are written to be read by one person
- are usually formal
- usually contain only text but as this is an estate agent may also contain images.

Business letters normally have a standard structure and should include:

- Business heading – in Azim's case this is pre-printed on the stationery but it used to be in a letter template. It includes the name, address, phone numbers, email address, etc. of the organisation. It also has a company logo.
- Date the letter was written – this can be placed on either side depending on the design of the business heading. In Azim's case it is on the left-hand side.
- Address of the recipient – usually placed on the left-hand side of the page below the heading.
- The salutation (greeting) – normally 'Dear Mr Jones', for example, or if the name is not known, then 'Dear Sir or Dear Madam' may be used. It is not appropriate to use the first name initial(s) (for example, Mr T Jones) when addressing in this way.
- Subject line – Azim usually adds a subject line stating what the letter is about.
- The ending – Azim usually adds 'Yours sincerely' when he knows the name of the person he is writing to, although he also uses 'Yours faithfully' where he starts the letter with 'Dear Sir or Madam'.
- Signature – Azim then adds his signature and printed name so that the recipient knows who he is, which in his case is very important as his signature is very hard to read.
- Azim also often has to add a copy list – this is a list of anyone else who is being sent a copy of the letter, and is written 'Cc: Jane Davidson, Pam Smith' etc. at the bottom of the letter.
- Enclosures – Azim also adds an enclosures list of documents if documents are enclosed – to let the recipient know that documents were included with the letter as he knows that they sometimes go missing!

A good business letter

Azim knows that the above letter-writing conventions must always be followed. His letter is expected to be professional so that the reader doesn't have to struggle to figure out where a piece of information might be, know what action they should take next, or work out who sent it – everything has to be found in its correct place and needs to be accurate in terms of content, spelling and grammar.

Knowing the rules of letter writing is, in that sense, the same as knowing the rules of page layout or web design – the format of the document should support and clarify the content.

Mail merge

Sometimes Azim needs to send out the same letter to a large number of people. He does this using a mail merge.

Mail merge is a way of placing content from a spreadsheet, database or table into a word-processed document. Mail merge is ideal for creating personalised form letters or labels instead of Azim having to edit the original letter several times to input different personalised information. As you can imagine, this can save him a lot of time as well as worry about accidentally changing some of the information for the new recipient.

In order to create a mail merge Azim needs two documents: the letter and a file containing the data or records. This file can take many forms, for example a spreadsheet, a database or even another text document that has a table in it.

As you can see business documents have a much more formal structure compared to the informal communication methods that you will be more accustomed to. Jamal Ali works in the local Eye Planet cinema. They do not write many formal letters, but with a large number of staff working at strange hours they often use memos.

Memos

A memo is a short note to someone else in the same organisation. For example, the estate agent staff. It can be hand written, printed out and delivered by hand.

```
┌─────────────────────────────────────────────┐
│                                              │
│   Memo                    YouBuy             │
│                                              │
│   To:                 From:                  │
│                                              │
│   Date:                                      │
│                                              │
│   Subject:                                   │
│   - - - - - - - - - - - - - - - - - - - -    │
│   Message:                                   │
│                                              │
└─────────────────────────────────────────────┘
```

Memos are written to be read by many people within an organisation and usually contain only text.

Memos are usually informal in style but most organisations have a set format to ensure that essential information – such as subject, date, sender's name and, when the organisation is very large, contact details – is not missed out. In Jamal's case they all know each other so this is not needed.

Case study: Cushington Ceramic Seals

Two of the members of staff working at Cushington Ceramic Seals are Greg Hanson and Phil Hidson.

The company is situated on the Cushington industrial estate. They are a large manufacturing company producing ceramic components for the space and aircraft industry. Most of the company's products are sold for military use.

The company sells products to other companies worldwide. They do not sell to the general public so their customers are always other businesses.

The company has to buy in a large number of parts, materials and components from other companies around the world. Keeping an accurate record of stock is very important as some of the materials, such as sapphires, are very expensive and other materials do not last long before having to be thrown away. Greg also keeps a very accurate record of their contacts in the companies they deal with.

Because of the high cost of materials the company uses what is called a just in time (JIT) system where they buy the materials and components just before they need them.

Business email messages

You may think that emails are informal but Greg at Cushington Ceramic Seals often needs to write formal emails. Although a chatty style may be suitable for personal emails, in business it is important to write clearly, and Greg knows that he should avoid the use of the abbreviations he would use to friends or in text messaging.

Greg knows that he must be careful not to use all capital letters as this is can be seen as the written equivalent of shouting. He also knows that if he does not include a subject and/or message text the mail could end up in the recipient's 'junk' folder.

Many organisations insist that business emails should follow a similar writing style to other business letters, although the layout is very different. In any case, the email should always end with a 'signature', which is a few lines of stored text giving the name, job title and contact details of the sender.

Most email software has a facility to store a signature which, once stored, can be added automatically to every outgoing email. This saves Greg a lot of time but a signature must be thoroughly checked for accuracy or it will always be inaccurate.

At the top of an email there is what is called a **header**. Greg is careful to make sure that the Subject line in the header of his business emails makes clear what the email is about. In business, people often receive and send many hundreds of emails, therefore having a sensible Subject line is very important. Greg usually adds some brief detail about what the email is about to the Subject line so that people receiving the email know what it is about before opening it. He also adds his own email as a Cc so that he receives a copy of the email on his other computer.

The header also contains the name and email address of the recipient in the 'To:...' box, plus a '**Cc**:...' box if you want to send a copy of the email to someone else.

The '**Bcc**:...' box is for sending a blind copy. Greg uses this if he wants to copy someone in, but doesn't want the main recipient(s) to know that he has also sent the email to that person. The email address of the Bcc recipient is kept confidential as it will not be visible to the main recipient.

Getting the spelling of the email address correct is very important – get it wrong by just one letter and the email won't arrive, and Greg would end up getting an error message.

As Greg often has to reply to an email he clicks on the Reply option. Sometimes there is more than one person copied into the email in which case he clicks on Reply All – this will ensure that all the original people other than the ones in the Bcc option receive his reply. Greg also has to make sure that there are no errors, such as misspellings or poor grammar, in his emails. He has to be aware of some basic email etiquette (sometimes referred to as 'netiquette').

Sometimes Greg has to forward an email. When he does this he adds a message to explain why he is forwarding the email and any action the person who is receiving it needs to take (or whether it is just being forwarded to keep the recipient informed).

Email etiquette

- Answer all the questions asked in received emails.
- Avoid long sentences.
- Be careful with formatting.
- Be concise and to the point.
- Do not copy a message or attachment without permission.

Key words

Header
Cc (Carbon copy)
Bcc (Blind carbon copy)

What you need to do ✓

When you need to send the same message to a number of people, for example to invite them to a meeting, multiple names can be entered into the To: box. Entering email addresses in the To: box generally means that the message either requires some action or a response from all the recipients. Sometimes you may wish to copy a person or people into the message so that they are kept informed, but do not need to take any action. When this is the case their email address should be entered into the Cc: box.

Use RE: and the original subject so the examiner can check that you have replied to the message you have been sent.

Make sure that the business emails that you produce are professional and follow correct structures:

- Business emails must follow normal business practices:
  - ➤ Use To, Cc and Bcc correctly.
  - ➤ Include a Subject line that clearly describes what the email is about.
  - ➤ Always mention there is an attachment so that the person is aware that there is one.
  - ➤ Zip large attachments.
  - ➤ Make your emails as clear as possible.
  - ➤ Only use appropriate language.

- Do not write in CAPITALS.
- Don't leave out the message thread.
- Read the email before sending it.
- Take care to select either rich text or HTML messages as some email accounts will only accept rich text.
- Use proper spelling, grammar and punctuation.
- Use proper structure and layout.
- Never disclose another person's email address without their permission (use Bcc instead of Cc if you need to hide their address) or use Bcc when you need to keep someone's email address confidential.

Greg also often adds an attachment to the email. Again he knows that it is important to name the attachment appropriately and he often also mentions that there is an attachment in the body of the email.

Sorting and filing emails

One feature of email programs that Greg must use for the business is folders. The folders he uses include an inbox, drafts, sent items and deleted messages folders. But to help organise the company's emails into easy categories he has also created other folders. Folders help him to categorise the business emails according to subject and importance. He also has separate folders for each company they deal with.

The email program Greg uses has an address book feature. This allows him to enter the most-often used addresses into a file for quick reference. His email program also has a nickname feature so that he only has to enter one word for an email, instead of the full address. The address book also links to other important business information including businesses' postal addresses, phone numbers and fax numbers.

Using the address book Greg can send messages to groups. Greg does this by creating a distribution list, also known as a mailing list, which is a collection of email addresses and allows you to email multiple people at the same time. A distribution list can contain a few addresses, or many. For example, Greg frequently sends messages to the marketing team, so he has created a distribution list – called 'Marketing Team' – that contains the email addresses of everyone in that team.

When Greg is on holiday or at weekends his email account sends out automatic replies saying when he will return to the office. Most email software has a facility to type in a message that will be sent automatically when emails are received. These messages might be used to confirm that the email has been received and that someone will deal with it within a certain time frame, or to inform senders that the person

they are trying to contact is out of the office. Greg sets up an automatic response whenever he is out of the office.

Hints and tips

You need to demonstrate a thorough understanding of the common and advanced tools and features of email software by using things such as Cc, Bcc and zipped attachments. You also need to demonstrate a thorough understanding of email etiquette, including business etiquette as Greg demonstrates in his business use of email.

Greg also uses other specialist formal documents.

Order forms

Order forms are needed to order materials for the company. These have been designed so that they capture all the information that the business needs.

Order forms normally have a standard structure and should include:

- name of customer
- address of customer
- delivery address
- items ordered – description or stock code of each type of item
- the quantity required
- method of payment
- phone number.

Invoices

Phil is a trained business manager and accountant and as such also has to collect the money for the goods sold. Cushington Ceramic Seals is a manufacturing company, not a shop, and companies who buy the goods pay when they receive an invoice not when they receive the goods.

An invoice is a bill sent to a customer after the goods have been delivered. When you buy something in a shop you will normally pay for it at the cash desk, and when you order something from a mail order company you are usually expected to pay for the goods before you receive them. If a business orders items, such as manufactured parts, the supplier will deliver the goods, then send an invoice, which should be paid within a stated time. In Phil's case this is one month. An invoice should have a business heading and logo.

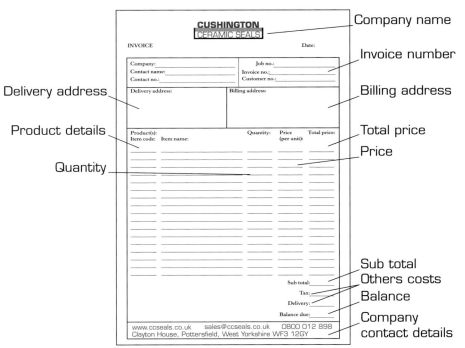

Phil does not produce flyers and articles for his business as his customers are business customers. But at the Eye Planet cinema Jamal produces a different range of documents to Phil. This is because their audiences are very different.

Articles

Jamal has responsibility for advertising. He uses a word processor to write an article for the local newspaper.

An article may be written for a national or local newspaper to advertise the films, or for magazines, newsletters and flyers. In style,

an article is something between a report and an essay. Jamal often adds a heading and one level of subheading.

Newsletters

Jamal also produces the cinema's newsletter.

A newsletter is a short version of a newspaper and they are often used by businesses to update their customers of their latest news. They are generally two to four pages in length but can be longer and can be either printed or presented digitally. They should include a mixture of images and text.

Many schools produce newsletters for their students and parents, keeping them up to date with new events and news about the school.

Newsletters can incorporate photos and graphical headings. They will often be laid out in columns or text boxes.

Advertisements

Alongside the newsletter Jamal has to produce advertisements.

A printed advertisement can be a page in a magazine, a single-sheet flyer, a leaflet, a poster or a website. They are carefully designed to catch the eye, and use logos that represent the product or organisation. Advertisements are always designed with a particular audience in mind. For the cinema, film lovers are the audience.

Poster

Posters are printed documents, usually designed to be eye catching and to give some basic information. They are usually displayed in public areas to advertise a particular product or service. Typically posters include both text and graphics. Anybody will be able to read Jamal's poster but he has to try and reach the audience he wants by writing the text and choosing images that he knows will appeal to them and by displaying the poster in certain places he knows they will visit.

Leaflet

Flyers and leaflets are meant for individuals so they are smaller than posters – often A5 (half an A4 page) in size. Jamal reaches his audience by posting them through letter-boxes and by handing them out in the cinema.

Jamal knows that leaflets must be both visual and informative. They should look attractive enough to encourage people to read them, but also deliver the information required.

Jamal designs the leaflets on one sheet of A4, printed on both sides (recto (front) and verso (back)) and folds them into several display panels of text with images. He needs to decide the best way to fold the leaflet before designing it.

V-fold

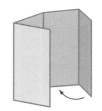

Roll fold
Has two or more parallel folds which fold in on each other.

Concertina fold
The paper zig-zags like a concertina.

C-fold

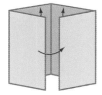

Open gate fold
The two parallel folds fold in to meet in the middle without overlapping.

Closed gate fold
The two parallel folds fold in to meet in the middle without over-lapping. Then the leaflet folds at the middle.

Leaflets can contain more information than other types of advertisement – but they should still be worded carefully and include appropriate graphics and headings. Leaflets are simple but effective promotional tools for businesses and other organisations. Uses include:

- advertising company information
- advertising single project information

■ targeted information from a business, for example a DIY store describing safety tips

■ targeted information from an organisation, for example the NHS giving support advice on a medical condition

■ promoting an event

■ publicising an action.

Leaflets are not necessarily read from front to back, beginning to end. People often pick them up and browse from the back or the middle, or glance at them quickly on their way to the bin. Therefore every section of a leaflet should be eye catching and informative.

Good leaflet	Bad leaflet
Business name and contact details clearly shown.	No contact details.
Good quality and relevant images to support the text.	Uses poor quality images, or none.
Headings and subheadings inform the reader of the following paragraph's content.	Confusing headings or lack of headings.
Organised into sections of coherent information under a heading or subheading.	Poorly organised with too much text that takes time to read.
Presents one message so the reader is clear about the point of the leaflet.	Presents too much information and is therefore confusing to the reader.

Hints and tips

You must create a range of appropriate documents using a range of file types. You must also select the appropriate method for the type of communication needed. This chapter shows a few of the more common methods.

What you need to do

You must be able to import information saved in a number of different formats into the most appropriate software packages and then format it appropriately for the purpose and audience. For example, a text file to display as formatted text, a table or a spreadsheet, or a csv file that needs to be imported into a database, word-processing package or a spreadsheet.

You must know how the software you are using handles the different file types. For example, in Microsoft Word a csv file can easily be converted into a table by using the 'convert text to table' option.

Reports

Dihana Simons works with Jamal at the cinema. She was asked to search for the most popular films from the last five years. She has done a large amount of research; what she now needs to do is put all of this information into a report.

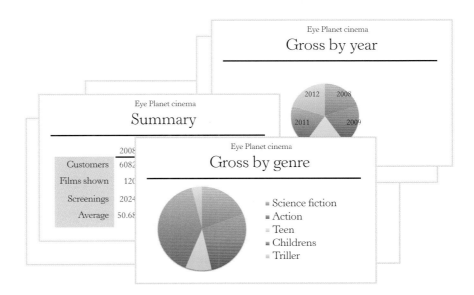

A report is any document that is written to explain a project, provide facts or generally convey information. Internal reports are used by managers to help them make decisions. Companies may also have to produce reports, such as an annual report, for the general public. Reports are usually written in a formal, structured style, with heavy use of headings, subheadings and numbered points. The type of report Dihana will produce will also be very different to the type of reports Greg has to write for his manufacturing company. This is because their audiences are very different. This changes the choice of design, text, colours and images; in fact it changes the whole look and feel of the document.

Reports:

- are written to be read by many people
- contain facts, findings and/or opinion
- can include images and graphics to demonstrate points and to show information graphically.

Dihana has found lots of information on the internet, sometimes it makes sense to reproduce the material from the source – but Dihana knows that she must check if she can use the content found and acknowledge her source or she could find herself and the business in

Key word

Creative Commons

court. Most of the information she finds says that it is licensed under **Creative Commons**. Many publishers on the web have a Creative Commons licence – they keep their copyright but allow people to copy and distribute their work provided they are given credit.

Good report	Bad report
• A report must have a clear logical structure – with clear signposting to show where the ideas are leading. • All reports must be written in good English – using short sentences and with correct grammar and spelling. • Avoid using capitals for emphasis – use bold, italics or underlines if you must. • Be consistent in how you format your headings – use predefined styles and modify these to suit your needs. • Defining a clear logical structure will make a report easier to write and to read. • Differentiate headings from the rest of the text by using bold, italics or underlines or by using a different font. But don't use too many of these in one document. • If you are using acronyms (a word that is formed by combining the first letters of other words) define them the first time you use them. • Only use capitals for proper nouns, place names, company names, etc. • A report must make a good first impression to the target audience. Correct presentation is very important.	• Bad spelling. • Figures and images not labelled descriptively and not referenced in the text. • No clear structure. • Tables not labelled or referenced in the text.

Jamal Ali looks after the electronic methods of advertising the cinema.

Information kiosks

In the foyer of the Eye Planet cinema there is an information kiosk.

An information kiosk is a digital presentation. It should run without anybody operating it. The information is mostly images with small amounts of text used to get a message across.

What you need to do ✓

Make sure that you fully record all of the required information:

■ Think about the audience:
  ➤ Select appropriate designs including fonts, colours and layout.
  ➤ Select the most appropriate document for the task.
■ Develop appropriate documents to present your solution:
  ➤ What do you want to say?
    ● What are the key points?

Websites

With so many young visitors and most teenagers using the internet, the cinema's presence on the internet is very important. Jamal uses the web to promote special offers.

A website is a collection of related web pages, each web page usually containing text, images and other digital media such as video or animation. Websites are hosted on a web server and accessed by users via the internet.

Typically a web page is a document which is written in plain text with formatting instructions in HTML that are interpreted by the user's web browser to display the page.

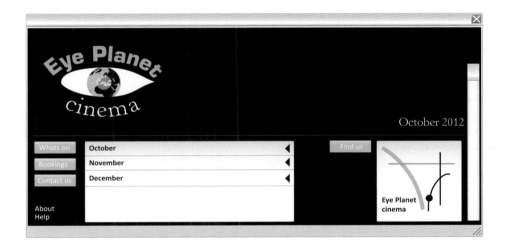

Planning and designing a web page

Before Jamal begins to create web-page content that is going to be read or viewed by other people he designs a web page and tests his design.

These are the questions in relation to designing a web page he asks himself:

- Who is my audience? – how will their age or knowledge of a subject affect what I write?
- How will the web page be used? – which format will be appropriate?
- What is the web page going to be doing? – what kind of information do I need to include?

Jamal develops his web page in a program called Adobe Dreamweaver although there are many other programs he could use.

Jamal has to add his content to the existing website so it must be consistent with the house style.

What you need to do ☑

Make sure that you think carefully about your web page:

- Is it appropriate?
  - ➤ Does it match the house style of the company?
  - ➤ Does it match the other pages?
  - ➤ Are the graphics of a suitable quality and size to download quickly?
- Check the web page:
  - ➤ Will it work in a range of browsers?
  - ➤ Does it download quickly?
  - ➤ Do all the links work?
  - ➤ Is it fit for purpose? – does it do what you set out to do?
  - ➤ Is it suitable for the target audience?
  - ➤ Is the text clear, accurate and free from errors (spelling and grammar)?

Next, Jamal:

- Sets up a suitable folder structure for the web page. He knows that he will need folders to store text files, the menu, images, etc.
- Writes some text to let people know about the films and includes suitable images making sure they are of good quality, in proportion and load quickly.
- Adds some graphics to make it appealing to the target audience.
- Makes good use of colour to make the page attractive and easy to read, avoiding colours that are difficult for colour-blind readers, for example red and green.
- Creates a button or link that takes the user to the menu. He knows that you must not forget that the user has to get back to the home page too! How will they do this?

Once Jamal has created his web page with the link to the home page, he tests that it is going to work in a browser.

Hints and tips

You will need to check that your web page works properly and as expected:

- Check that your web page looks as expected when it runs on another computer. It is a common mistake not to put all your files in the same folder. If your files are in different folders, when you test the web page on other machines some of the images might not appear.
- Get someone else to test your web page so that they can give you feedback, for example on whether they think it is attractive, has clear information and is easy to follow/navigate.

House style

It is important that a website is consistent in its layout and presentation of information from page to page. Deciding upon font types, colours and sizes, etc. are just a few things to consider. A house style guide can even cover preferred spellings. What background colours will you use? How will you size the images? How will the pages be set out? The key to creating a good website is to create a good house style. All a company's documents – from websites to publicity leaflets – should follow the house style – this will make them all look similar and present to the reader a consistent company image. By making it consistent, the website will look better and be easier to use. Jamal has to follow the cinema's rules on house style.

Using images

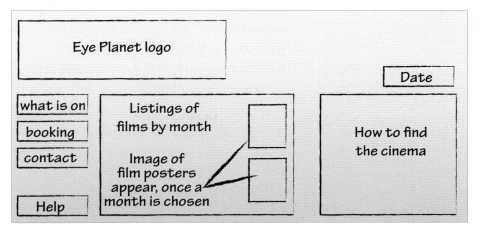

Jamal needs to put a number of pictures of upcoming films on the website. But he knows that they need to be the correct size. The images he has are very large and would take a very long time to download in a browser. First, he needs to resize them using a graphics program.

Resizing an image

Digital images are made up of a huge number of individual dots called pixels (the word pixel is short for 'picture element'). Every digital image is a rectangle (or square) which can be measured in terms of pixel width and height. Digital cameras are often referred to in terms of their 'megapixel' capability – this means how many million pixels are in a photo.

Jamal also knows that an image with a set number of pixels can still appear to be a different size on different computer monitors. This is because monitors themselves have their own resolution.

First Jamal zooms in to each image.

Zoom

A common mistake is to view an image and think the size is fine, when in fact the image is much larger or smaller than it appears. This can happen when your viewing program automatically resizes the image to fit the available screen space. Jamal views the image and makes sure it is set to '100%' or 'actual size'. Images that are too large create very large file sized documents and images that are too small can look pixelated and out of focus when zoomed in.

What size does the image need to be?

Exactly how big you want the image to be will depend on its intended use. Jamal knows that for a web page, the image obviously needs to fit the space available.

- Web page photos are usually anywhere between 100 pixels wide (large thumbnail size) and 800 pixels (the full width of many monitors). An average photo might be 300 pixels wide.
- Email attachments for casual viewing should normally be between 200 pixels and 600 pixels wide.
- Images that are intended for print usually require 300 pixels per inch when printed.

Jamal has two ways to change the image's size – **Crop** and **Resize**. He often uses both methods depending on the situation. He will usually crop the image first and then resize it.

Crop the image

Using the rectangular selection tool, Jamal selects the area of the image he wishes to keep, then selects the crop option. Cropping removes some of the content Jamal does not want.

Resize the image

In the program menu, Jamal selects the option to resize – a window appears which allows him to enter width and height values for the image. He adjusts these values and clicks 'OK'. Jamal maintains the aspect ratio (proportion) of the image – his software allows him to do this by adjusting the width and height at the same time.

Apply the skills you have learnt about using images to any documents you produce – not just to web pages.

Hints and tips

Use folders to store your work and all the associated files and images used. Remember to follow copyright rules.

	Good web page	Bad web page
Backgrounds	• Clear and easy to read text on a simple background. • Matches the rest of the website.	• Colour combinations of text and background that make the text hard to read. • Default grey colour or distracting backgrounds that make the text hard to read.
General design	• Good use of house style. Every web page looks like it belongs to the same website – there are repeated elements that have been added to all of the pages in the same place on each page. • Good use of images, subheadings and quotes to break up large areas of text. • Page downloads quickly. • Page fits into 800 x 600 pixel space.	• Frames that make you scroll sideways. • Lack of contrast. • No focal point on the page. • Page does not fit within standard browser window (800 x 600 pixels). • Pages that do not load in some browsers. • Too many focal points on the page.
Text	• Background does not interrupt the text. • Text is big enough to read, but not too big. • The order of information is perfectly clear.	• Paragraphs of type in all capitals. • Paragraphs of type in bold and/or italic. • Text crowding against the left edge. • Text that is too small to read. • Text that stretches all the way across the page.
Links	• Link colours coordinate with page colours. • Links are underlined so they are instantly clear to the visitor or are contained in graphic buttons.	• Blue link borders around graphics. • Dead links (links that don't work any more). • Default blue links. • Links that are not clear about where they will take you.
Navigation	• Navigation buttons and bars are easy to understand and use. • Navigation buttons and bars provide the visitor with a clue as to where they are and what page of the site they are currently on. • Navigation is consistent throughout the website.	• Complicated frames, too many frames, unnecessary scroll bars in frames. • Unclear navigation, over-complex navigation. • Useless page titles that don't explain what the page is about.
Graphics	• Animated graphics do not keep running and turn off by themselves. • Buttons are not too big. • Every graphic has an alternative label. • Graphics and backgrounds use browser-safe colours.	• Graphics that don't fit on the screen (assuming a screen of 800 x 600 pixels). • Large graphic files that take a long time to load. • Meaningless or useless graphics. • Missing graphics.

Copying and pasting images and text from the internet

Dihana browses a website for an image she would like to copy. Dihana remembers that before copying any text or images, she must check who owns the copyright, and if she is allowed to use it. Once she is happy she is allowed to copy her chosen image, she selects the image by clicking on it and then right clicks the mouse and selects Copy. She goes to her document and right clicks the mouse again and this time, clicks Paste.

Sometimes Dihana simply right clicks the mouse on the image and selects Save image (selecting her user area to store the images in appropriate folders). She does this when she wants to collect images for use later.

Dihana always chooses an image that can be made bigger or cropped and still be of high enough quality but she also knows that it must have a reasonable file size or the document or presentation will be too large. As such she chooses an image format such as jpeg which uses compression.

To resize the image Dihana selects the image by clicking on it and when she sees the handles appear at the corners she selects and uses the corners to resize the image retaining its shape. She knows that if she uses the horizontal or vertical selectors she will distort the image.

From the same website, Dihana selects a section of text by highlighting it with her mouse. She then follows the same procedure as for the image to copy and paste it into her document.

There are lots of different ways to make documents look more interesting by organising text and images so that they are well presented and by formatting documents to make particular points stand out. Using tables is a good way of organising information in a document. In some cases, presenting information as a chart or graph makes it easier for the audience to understand.

Dihana is asked to present her findings to the management team.

Presentations

Dihana decides to use a slide show to display her information through animation, images and sound. Her presentation will be displayed to a particular audience. She knows that she must only display the key messages in her slideshow and present the details another way.

A presentation is a combination of live talk and ready-prepared graphical materials (a slide show). The alternative could be a video on its own, or a simple talk without illustrations.

Presentations:

- are written to be seen by many people in the same room
- contain slides that can be displayed on a screen
- contain images and graphics to demonstrate points
- show the main findings only (more information is given in the presenter's accompanying talk).

Combining graphical visuals and speech into one presentation has a number of advantages:

- The slides add impact to a talk – the audience is much more likely to listen and understand if the message is reinforced by text and pictures.

- Dihana can feel confident that the main points of her talk are included.
- Dihana can take the presentation at her own speed.
- Dihana can respond to the audience as the presentation proceeds, going back to earlier slides if necessary.

Presentations differ according to how they will be viewed:

- Projecting from a computer – Dihana connects a projector to her laptop. This projects onto a screen whatever is shown on the computer monitor. She is able to face the audience while controlling the presentation.
- Dihana's presentation can be viewed directly on a computer screen – a large display screen can be added as a second monitor, so she can still control the presentation from her laptop. For a presentation to a couple of people it is possible to simply view it on a computer's normal monitor.

Both methods display the output from a computer in real time. This means that the presentation can include animation and video. It can also include sound, provided that suitable speakers have been installed.

To achieve a good presentation, Dihana must show that she understands who she is producing the presentation for and what the purpose of it is. Everything she includes should keep the audience and purpose in mind.

Sometimes Dihana has to produce 'self-running' presentations to run in the foyer of Eye Planet and advertising type presentations designed to be viewed on a computer screen. For the presentations for the foyer, timings are very important.

What is the purpose?	• What does she want to achieve? • What message does she want to get across? • Who is her target audience?
How should she plan the presentation?	• Decide what she wants to say. • Decide what to put on the slides to illustrate her points. • Limit the number of slides. • Decide how many images and graphics she wants to add.

Dihana must also keep the design consistent. To do this she will consider text size and font and whether the information needs to be read from a distance or not.

She carefully selects just the information she needs from the notes she made. She probably won't need all the information available – just the key points that help get her message across in a way that is appropriate for her audience.

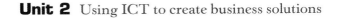

While Dihana is doing a presentation to a group she uses speaker notes to help her remember what to say. She also gives these to people attending her talk, this way her colleagues can view and edit the notes.

Speaker notes are simply that – notes for a speaker! They are short notes of key points to be used as a reminder while giving a speech.

For example, when Dihana is using Microsoft PowerPoint she makes a note of the main points of each slide to remind her of what she is going to say when she is presenting it. Her notes remind her of additional information to help her talk around the bullet points on the slide. Speaker notes should only include short notes/comments, not a script of the whole presentation/speech.

Dihana also knows that when she is selecting images, they must be relevant to the text on her presentation. She needs to consider the number of images she will use to make sure that her slides do not get too crowded and make sure that she does not stretch and distort the images.

Good presentation	Bad presentation
A minimum number of slides and no more than ten for a five-minute talk.	Too many slides.
All elements, even figure legends, are visible from the back of the audience.	Text too small or too much text.
Animation is used on content – video or introducing ideas one by one.	Too much animation.
Good organisation – introduction with overview, discussion and conclusion.	Poor organisation with no structure.
Images rather than text – use relevant graphics to illustrate points.	Irrelevant graphics and images.
Lists of three bullet points – audiences remember threes.	Long lists with irrelevant information.
No more than one idea per slide.	Too many ideas per slide.
Spellchecked and grammatically correct.	Lots of errors.

Animation effects

Dihana knows that adding movement to her presentation slides will be exciting, but carries with it some risk. Two of the most common ways to add movement are by animating a slide element such as text or a graphic and by using movement to bring a new slide on screen (called

What you need to do ☑

Make sure that any presentations you produce are appropriate for business use:

- Sensible balance between text and images.
- Not too much text on each slide. Use short bullet points.
- Not too many animations.
- Uses sensible slide effects – think about slide animation effects and transitions.
- Contains consistent formatting:
  - ➤ Each slide must follow a house style – use master slides to achieve this.
- Make sure text is large enough to be viewed from the back of the room.
- Contains speaker notes – these should be brief notes which contain the essential points to help the speaker to talk around the bullet points on the slide.
- Check that the animations work as intended.

Key word

Exporting

slide transition). She has to keep in mind that when using movement effects she should not be distracting the audience from her message.

There are two key points to consider when using animation effects. The first is the finishing point, which is the position that the slide element (such as text or a graphic) ends up in – this is where Dihana wants the audience to see the text or graphic when the movement effect is finished. The second is the starting point, which is the position from where the slide element starts the movement effect. She knows that in general, the longer it takes for the slide element to get from the starting point to the finishing point, the harder it is for the audience to understand the message she is trying to deliver.

Slide transitions

As well as designing slides where elements move, Dihana can add slide transitions where the elements stay where they are but the slide fades in or out. A transition is the movement from one slide to another, whereas an animation is the movement of individual elements (lines of text and/or graphics) on a slide.

Copyright

One of the most important things Dihana has to remember is copyright. How is she going to use the information she has chosen and will this be within the law?

Finally, has she checked her information to make sure it's spelt correctly and makes sense?

To use data produced by another application

The ability to import data is very important in software applications because it means that one application can complement another. Many programs are designed to be able to import graphics in a variety of formats.

The opposite of importing is **exporting**, which refers to the ability of one application to format data for use in another application.

Sometimes Dihana has to import text. She can copy text from other documents but copied text keeps its original formatting. Importing text from a plain text file allows her to format the text how she wants. If she wants to keep the original formatting she imports the text using RTF (Rich Text Format) or enhanced text format.

Of course this works both ways. If she wants to keep the formatting of her own document when she exports text she must use RTF or enhanced text.

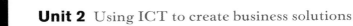

6

Types of business software spreadsheets

Understanding and formatting spreadsheets

Spreadsheets are used for calculating with numbers and presenting the results of those calculations in a visual format. They are used, for example, by accountants, engineers, bankers, scientists, sales representatives, supermarkets, market researchers and teachers. In fact, anyone who needs to make calculations on profit/loss, financial forecasts, manufacturing designs, results from experiments, sales, commission, data analysis, keeping track of pupil presence and marks, and for many other tasks.

Jane Morrison at the estate agents creates a spreadsheet by first importing data that has been exported from a word-processed list saved as a CSV file.

You can import any of these file formats into a spreadsheet:

csv	xls	xlsx	txt	ods	tsv	tsb

Case study: SaverShop supermarket

Naomi Johnson works at the SaverShop supermarket. Naomi has been asked to look after the ice cream and cold drinks stand at the front of the shop. She needed to explore how to make a profit.

Naomi has to decide whether to use a spreadsheet or database for her data. She knows that this choice depends upon the nature of the data analysis required. Naomi knows that spreadsheets are designed to work with numbers. Most of the data she needs to analyse is numerical, but her spreadsheet package can also act as a simple flat-file database. Although it is not as easy to use as a specialised database package she knows it is adequate for her simple tasks. She also knows the database functions in her spreadsheets will be enough for her needs to search and sort data she will have on ice creams and cold drinks.

▶ What you will learn

Spreadsheet development skills:

- Enter data into a spreadsheet
- Import data using CSV for text files
- Format data (for example, number, alignment, font type, font colour, fill colours, borders)
- Edit cells (merge, split cells, add or delete columns and rows)
- Make good use of page layout, gridlines and headings
- Use of functions and formulae
- Change data to model outcomes

Hints and tips

You will need to show that you can import data into a spreadsheet and database and that you work with accuracy. Your spreadsheets and databases must fully meet the specified requirements of the business, so be careful to identify these first.

She knows that the choice between database and spreadsheet depends on:

- how many records she will be entering (she does not have many)
- how the company will use the data (she will be the only user)
- if she needs to control how the data is entered (it is her decision)
- who is going to use the data (only her)
- if she needs to perform automatic calculations (she will need to do this)
- if she wants to create charts and graphs from the data (she will need to do this)
- if she wants to ask 'what if' questions (she will need to do this).

In this example Naomi has only 20 products to enter. She needs to track product names and sales information. By asking herself the above questions, she knows that she has a small number of records, is the only person who needs to use the data, does not need to control how the data is entered and needs to produce charts and graphs. A spreadsheet is clearly the best choice for her needs.

Naomi had no digital data to import and had to create the spreadsheet from scratch.

Naomi uses formatting to change the appearance of the text and graphical elements. This includes things such as the font style and size, bold, italics, margins, etc. Equally important is editing the content to make sure that what is being said meets the needs of the audience. Part of good editing also involves careful organisation of text, images and charts.

Naomi wanted to collect data on how much milkshake was sold in one week. The table below shows the results sorted by day.

Day	Chocolate	Strawberry	Vanilla	Total	Unit price	Total
Mon	53	78	126		£1.55	
Tue	72	97	87		£1.55	
Wed	112	73	86		£1.55	
Thu	33	78	143		£1.55	
Fri	76	47	162		£1.55	

All spreadsheets basically consist of a grid of what are called **cells**. The cells are made up of columns and rows. The **columns** are labelled across the top, usually from A to Z, and then from AA to AZ and so on. The **rows** are numbered down the side.

Each cell in the spreadsheet can be uniquely identified by its **cell address**, which is the intersection of the column and row. For example, the first cell in column A is called A1. The 29th cell in column H is H29. When you click in a cell, you will see its address displayed in the address box, usually near the top left of the window.

You can also refer to a **cell range** by specifying the first and last cells in the range, separated by a colon. Thus, L12:R19 refers to a range of cells starting in column L, row 12 and extending to column R, row 19.

Column ⎯
Cell ref ⎯
Row ⎯
Cell ⎯

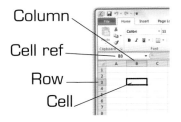

What makes a good spreadsheet?

Two things: good design and good data.

This may sound obvious, but it's all too easy to dive into creating a spreadsheet without putting much thought into its design. And a poorly designed spreadsheet is bound to make it harder to enter valid data.

Naomi knows that good design doesn't just mean making your spreadsheet look good by formatting the data. She knows that good spreadsheet design also consists of organising the data logically and ensuring that all her formulae are correct.

Using simple formulae

To save you adding up data in cells there is a simple function that does this for us called AutoSum. You will see an icon on your toolbar that looks like this: Σ.

Highlight the cell where you want your answer and double click on the Σ icon.

Here are some examples of other calculations you may come across:

```
= cellref + cellref

= cellref - cellref

= cellref * cellref

= cellref / cellref
```

When you type in the calculation, make sure you are in the cell where you want the answer to be displayed.

Normal view and formula view

Your spreadsheet by default is set as normal view, which means it shows the data exactly as it is entered. However, it is sometimes useful when using formulae to see the actual formula itself to show how it works. This can be done with a simple toolbar button or keyboard combination.

Again, what makes a good spreadsheet?

Think about it! What considerations do you need to take into account when producing your spreadsheet? Think about the layout and presentation. Is the formatting of your data consistent? Do your graphs and charts accurately represent the data? Have you tested your spreadsheet to see if it works as intended?

Case study: Ben's Dental Surgery

Ben Clark at Ben's Dental Surgery also uses spreadsheets but these are more complex and have more than one user. Ben starts by setting up a simple spreadsheet to calculate the profits on dental products sold.

Look at Ben's spreadsheet below and make a note of the formatting techniques used. Can you think of any others that could be used? He has also added some formatting to the cells.

	Date	Expenditure	Refund	Total expen	Income	Profit
1	Date	Expenditure	Refund	Total expen	Income	Profit
2	03-Jun	£498.00	£12.00	£486.00	£4,234.00	£3,748.00
3	05-Jul	£334.00	£80.00	£254.00	£9,798.00	£9,544.00
4	09-Aug	£567.00		£567.00	£7,657.00	£7,090.00
5	02-Sep	£987.00	£106.00	£881.00	£6,012.00	£5,131.00
6	06-Oct	£456.00		£456.00	£6,412.00	£5,956.00
7	08-Nov	£877.00	£76.00	£801.00	£4,078.00	£3,277.00
8	01-Dec	£433.00	£12.00	£421.00	£7,456.00	£7,035.00
9	01-Jan	£498.00		£498.00	£4,234.00	£3,736.00
10	03-Feb	£334.00	£80.00	£254.00	£8,798.00	£8,544.00
11	07-Mar	£567.00	£122.00	£445.00	£7,657.00	£7,212.00
12	02-Apr	£987.00	£176.00	£811.00	£4,012.00	£3,201.00
13	01-May	£456.00	£4.00	£452.00	£8,412.00	£7,960.00
14						
15	Totals	£6,994.00	£668.00	£6,326.00	£78,760.00	£72,434.00

Ben has used formulae to deduct the refund from the expenditure in the total expenditure column. He has also used formulae to calculate the profit and totals.

Constructing formulae

Ben uses simple formulae in his spreadsheet using the mathematical operators:

+ pronounced 'plus' and used for adding

– pronounced 'minus' and used for taking away

* pronounced 'star' or 'multiplied by' and used for multiplying

/ pronounced 'slash' or 'divided by' and used for dividing

Functions

Rather than adding up each cell using a mathematical operator Ben use the term **SUM**. This is a function. You use functions to perform calculations on data. Spreadsheets have built-in functions to make them easier to use – but you do have to understand what they do exactly. Functions can be built into formulae. For example:

```
=SUM(B2:D2)*(F2)
```

The AutoSUM function adds a sum function to the spreadsheet that will add up a row or column of figures. The AutoSum button is in the main toolbar and looks like a Greek capital sigma, Σ.

Unfortunately Ben made an error in his spreadsheet. He did not realise that refunds are paid by a French supplier in euros. He modifies his spreadsheet to automatically convert from euros to pounds.

Spreadsheets can be used to predict what might happen when things change. Ben needs to model what would happen to the profit if the expenditure went up by 10%. Ben also notices that there is a formatting error in cell D15 as it shows the total in euros not in pounds, he changes the format of the whole column so that the error will not occur again when he adds data in new rows. His spreadsheet now looks like the one at the top of page 181.

Cell referencing

Because Ben needs the exchange rate to be applied to all of his converted calculations he uses the '$' sign before the row reference to make it an absolute cell reference. Ben has put the exchange rate in a single absolute cell, J2. Whenever he needs to make a calculation involving the exchange rate he can simply reference this cell. If the exchange rate is changed, then he only needs to update one figure and in all of the cells that use this cell reference the formulae would automatically update to reflect the

Key word

SUM

What you need to do ☑

Remember that spreadsheets need to be designed:

- Think about design, text formatting and layout.
- Consider data input and output.
- Use sensible formulae that produce the correct results.
- Layout the spreadsheet effectively so calculations can be made efficiently.

	A	B	C	D	E	F	G	H	I	J
1	Date	Expenditure	Refund	Converted	Total expenditure	Income	Profit			
2	03-Jun	£498.00	€12.00	£9.92	£488.08	£4,234.00	£3,745.92		Exchange rate	1.21
3	05-Jul	£334.00	€80.00	£66.12	£267.88	£9,798.00	£9,530.12			
4	09-Aug	£567.00			£567.00	£7,657.00	£7,090.00			
5	02-Sep	£987.00	€106.00	£87.60	£899.40	£6,012.00	£5,112.60			
6	06-Oct	£456.00			£456.00	£6,412.00	£5,956.00			
7	08-Nov	£877.00	€76.00	£62.81	£814.19	£4,078.00	£3,263.81			
8	01-Dec	£433.00	€12.00	£9.92	£423.08	£7,456.00	£7,032.92			
9	01-Jan	£498.00			£498.00	£4,234.00	£3,736.00			
10	03-Feb	£334.00	€80.00	£66.12	£267.88	£8,798.00	£8,530.12			
11	07-Mar	£567.00	€122.00	£100.83	£466.17	£7,657.00	£7,190.83			
12	02-Apr	£987.00	€176.00	£145.45	£841.55	£4,012.00	£3,170.45			
13	01-May	£456.00	€4.00	£3.31	£452.69	£8,412.00	£7,959.31			
14										
15	Totals	£6,994.00	€ 668.00	£552.07	£6,441.93	£78,760.00	£72,318.07			
16										

change. But this type of reference could be linked to any cell. The reason Ben used an absolute cell reference is because he knows that he will need to copy and paste rows of formulae to add new dates.

Let's look at this in a little more detail. In most spreadsheets by default, cell references are **relative**. This means that when you copy a formula from one cell to another it will amend the cell references in the pasted formulae. When Ben copies the formula from one row to add it to another the formula updates to suit the new row.

For example, if you write =A1+A2 in cell A3 then copy and paste it into B3, the formula will be changed automatically to =B1+B2. The formula is relative to where you paste it and this is why it is called **relative cell referencing**.

If you want to keep a reference to the original cells, A1 and A2, you need to use **absolute cell referencing**. Absolute cell referencing is done with dollar signs. In this example, =$A$1+$A$2.

In the same way, Ben always wants the calculation to be based upon one specified cell so he must make his formulae absolute. Let's look at Ben's spreadsheet in formulae view.

Key words

Relative
Relative cell referencing
Absolute cell referencing

	A	B	C	D	E	F	G	H	I	J
1	Date	Expenditure	Refund	Converted	Total expenditure	Income	Profit			
2	41063	498	12	=C2/$J$2	=B2-D2	4234	=F2-E2		Exchange rate	1.21
3	41095	334	80	=C3/$J$2	=B3-D3	9798	=F3-E3			
4	41130	567	0	=C4/$J$2	=B4-D4	7657	=F4-E4			
5	41154	987	106	=C5/$J$2	=B5-D5	6012	=F5-E5			
6	41188	456	0	=C6/$J$2	=B6-D6	6412	=F6-E6			
7	41221	877	76	=C7/$J$2	=B7-D7	4078	=F7-E7			
8	41244	433	12	=C8/$J$2	=B8-D8	7456	=F8-E8			
9	40909	498	0	=C9/$J$2	=B9-D9	4234	=F9-E9			
10	40942	334	80	=C10/$J$2	=B10-D10	8798	=F10-E10			
11	40975	567	122	=C11/$J$2	=B11-D11	7657	=F11-E11			
12	41001	987	176	=C12/$J$2	=B12-D12	4012	=F12-E12			
13	41030	456	4	=C13/$J$2	=B13-D13	8412	=F13-E13			
14										
15	Totals	6994	=SUM(C2:C13)	=SUM(D2:D13)	=SUM(E2:E13)	=SUM(F2:F13)	=SUM(G2:G13)			

If you look at column D you will see that he has used an absolute cell reference to J2, so any changes he makes in this cell will automatically change the calculations in columns E and G in addition to column D.

Types of business software spreadsheets

The spreadsheet created by Ben is for a single dental surgery and four dentists work in the practice. They share the cost of rent, rates and staff (two dental nurses and a receptionist). Ben creates a spreadsheet of these costs, which are called fixed costs or overheads, so that each of the four dentists can pay an equal amount for them.

	A	B	C	D
1	Overheads			
2		Month	Annual	
3	Wages	£4,250.00	£51,000.00	
4	Rent	£2,800.00	£33,600.00	
5	Phone	£127.78	£1,533.36	
6	Rates	£1,370.00	£16,440.00	
7	Heating	£400.00	£4,800.00	
8	Totals	£8,947.78	£107,373.36	
9				
10	Charge per Dentist	£26,843.34		
11				

He can then combine the expenditure/profit data for each dentist into a single spreadsheet to deduct the shared charge from the totals to give the annual income (before tax) for each dentist.

	A	B	C	D	E
1	Date	Dentist One	Dentist Two	Dentist Three	Dentist Four
2	03-Jun	£3,745.92	£3,745.92	£6,745.92	£3,745.92
3	05-Jul	£9,530.12	£5,530.12	£8,530.12	£9,530.12
4	09-Aug	£7,090.00	£5,090.00	£6,090.00	£7,220.00
5	02-Sep	£5,112.60	£6,552.60	£5,112.60	£5,555.60
6	06-Oct	£5,956.00	£5,956.00	£5,956.00	£9,956.00
7	08-Nov	£3,263.81	£3,263.81	£7,263.81	£9,263.81
8	01-Dec	£7,032.92	£7,032.92	£4,032.92	£7,032.92
9	01-Jan	£3,736.00	£3,736.00	£3,736.00	£5,736.00
10	03-Feb	£8,530.12	£4,530.12	£8,530.12	£8,530.12
11	07-Mar	£7,190.83	£6,190.83	£2,190.83	£7,190.83
12	02-Apr	£3,170.45	£7,170.45	£3,170.45	£8,170.45
13	01-May	£7,959.31	£5,459.31	£7,959.31	£4,959.31
14					
15	Totals	£72,318.07	£64,258.07	£69,318.07	£86,891.07
16	Net	£45,474.73	£37,414.13	£42,474.73	£60,047.73

We can see how this shared charge is deducted by looking at the spreadsheet in formula view:

	A	B	C	D	E
14					
15	Totals	=SUM(B1:B13)	=SUM(C1:C13)	=SUM(D1:D13)	=SUM(E1:E13)
16	Net	=B15-$B27	=C15-$B27	=D15-$B27	=E15-$B27
17					
18	Overheads				
19		Month	Annual		
20	Wages	4250	=B20*12		
21	Rent	2800	=B21*12		
22	Phone	127.78	=B22*12		
23	Rates	1370	=B23*12		
24	Heating	400	=B24*12		
25	Totals	=SUM(B20:B24)	=B25*12		
26					
27	Charge per Dentist	=C25/4			
28					

Notice in the formulae in row 16 how Ben has used the '$' sign to make cell B27 an absolute cell reference for when he wants to add new dentists and copy the columns and formulae.

Ben needs to use the spreadsheet to model changes in costs. The dentists want to know what will happen to profits if prices rise by different amounts of inflation. Ben adds further calculations to the spreadsheet.

	A	B	C	D	E	F
14						
15	Totals	£72,318.08	£64,258.08	£69,318.08	£86,891.08	
16	Net	£63,146.61	£55,086.61	£60,146.61	£77,719.61	
17						
18	Overheads					
19		Month	Annual			
20	Wages	4250	51000			
21	Rent	2800	33600			
22	Phone	127.78	1533.36			
23	Rates	1370	16440			
24	Heating	400	4800			
25	Totals	£8,947.78	107373.36	Inflation	10.00%	
26				Inflation Total	£894.78	
27	Charge per	£9,171.47				
28						

Now Ben can add any inflation in the cell E26 and it will update the net for each dentist. If we look at this in formulae view we can see how Ben achieved this in his spreadsheet.

	A	B	C	D	E
14					
15	Totals	=SUM(B1:B13)	=SUM(C1:C13)	=SUM(D1:D13)	=SUM(E1:E13)
16	Net	=B15-$B27	=C15-$B27	=D15-$B27	=E15-$B27
17					
18	Overheads				
19		Month	Annual		
20	Wages	4250	=B20*12		
21	Rent	2800	=B21*12		
22	Phone	127.78	=B22*12		
23	Rates	1370	=B23*12		
24	Heating	400	=B24*12		
25	Totals	=SUM(B20:B24)	=B25*12	Inflation	0.1
26				Inflation Total	=B25*E25
27	Charge per Dentist	=B25+E26/4			

Of course this is quite a simple model and Ben could go on to add other variables and more complex rules to explore other variables. The dentists could increase their prices in line with inflation and it would be quite simple for Ben to add this to his model using the same inflation absolute cell reference.

	A	B	C	D	E	F
14						
15	Totals	£72,318.08	£64,258.08	£69,318.08	£86,891.08	
16	Net	£45,474.74	£37,414.74	£42,474.74	£60,047.74	
17						
18	Overheads					
19		Month	Annual			
20	Wages	4250	51000			
21	Rent	2800	33600			
22	Phone	127.78	1533.36			
23	Rates	1370	16440			
24	Heating	400	4800			
25	Totals	£8,947.78	107373.36	Inflation	30.00%	
26				Inflation Total	£2,684.33	
27	Charge per Dentist	26843.34				

What you need to do ☑

Remember to use a spreadsheet whenever numerical data needs to be modelled or sorted:

- Think about how formulae can be used to calculate new information from the data.
- Use relative and absolute cell referencing appropriately.
- Copy and paste repeated formulae.
- Check the accuracy of your data.
- Model data to make predictions.

Using formulae in spreadsheets

Naomi started with a paper-based record of how many ice creams were sold in the month of June, including the prices and which were the best selling flavours.

We explored her spreadsheet earlier but now she wants to produce a chart to show the best selling ice creams. This will go into the next issue of the company newsletter.

Although Naomi could simply use a spreadsheet to set up simple tables of textual information, as we have seen before, a spreadsheet's real usefulness lies in its ability to calculate using formulae – and to recalculate automatically when values change. Naomi also knows that spreadsheets are ideal when you want to produce a graph to display data. Spreadsheets are great for budgets, financial statements and other tasks that require calculations and/or graphs.

Like Ben, Naomi created a spreadsheet model. A model is a 'simulation' or representation of a business system. For example, Naomi's model shows the costs of the ingredients and the actual sales of ice creams in the previous month so that she can use this data to predict the profits for the following month, by changing some of the data or the formulae. Models are based upon 'rules' (which is how the formulae are written) and 'data' from previous experience or predictions. Models can be simple or complex. For example, Naomi could create a complex spreadsheet model to predict the weather so that she could predict ice cream sales in the future, but it would require a large amount of past weather data and a number of complicated formulae.

Because Naomi cannot create this weather model she can only base her model on what happened last week or month; if there is very hot or cold weather in the following month the sales of ice cream will change and so will the profits. She decides that building a model on last year's sales data would be better than last month's as it will be closer to predicted sales this year than just looking at last month.

Hints and tips

When using formulae and functions to make things easier and quicker, make sure they work properly! Do a random check of one of the answers and see if it's as expected.

Don't forget these are important files so make a backup of your work regularly on separate media, for example using a USB memory stick.

The accuracy of any model depends upon the accuracy of the data that is entered and the formulae used, but it also depends on how easy it is to base what will happen in the future on what has happened in the past.

The main advantage of computer models to a business is that they can allow 'what if' questions to be asked. For example, Naomi can see how changes in the weather have affected past sales and she can change the predicted number of ice creams sold or the price of an ice cream. She can use the model to see what could happen if it is very hot next week for example. She knows that the ingredients are expensive and do not last for long so to make a profit she must model what is needed as accurately as possible.

Once a model has been created, searching and sorting data also becomes very important.

Naomi often needs to organise the spreadsheet so that it is easy to explore the data in a chosen sequence, for example by flavour of ice cream. This is called sorting. It is possible in all spreadsheet programs to sort a range of cells alphabetically or numerically by any row or column.

Spreadsheet development skills

As we have seen, Ben's needs are quite different from Naomi's, but they can both benefit by using a spreadsheet.

Ben was never much good at maths and as the totals are important to the dentists, Ben uses a spreadsheet to calculate all of them, but Ben also needs to perform more complex tasks where a spreadsheet can prove useful.

To carry out these complex tasks Ben needs to use more complex functions. These make his spreadsheet calculate important data for the running of the dental practice and automatically tell him if stock levels run below a critical level. Ben uses an IF function to do this on his stock spreadsheet.

IF function

The IF function is used to find out if the data in a cell is 'true' or 'false'. If it's true, one thing happens; if it's false, a different thing happens. The test looks like this:

```
=IF(logical _ test, value _ if _ true, value _ if _ false)
```

Ben also has to keep track of payments to external companies and again he uses an IF function. Let's take a look at one of these spreadsheets in more detail to see how he uses this function.

	A	B	C	D	E	F
1	Order Date	Customer	Terms	Due Date	Paid Date	Status
2	03/01/2012	Redbridge	30	02/02/2012	02/03/2012	Paid
3	04/02/2012	Cushington	30	05/03/2012	08/04/2012	Paid
4	05/03/2012	French	10	15/03/2012	08/04/2012	Paid
5	06/03/2013	Kingsley	30	05/04/2013	04/04/2012	Paid
6	07/03/2012	Fill	30	06/04/2012		LATE
7	08/03/2012	DentMark	10	18/03/2012	28/03/2012	Paid
8	10/03/2012	Redbridge	30	09/04/2012		LATE
9	10/03/2012	Cushington	30	09/04/2012	17/03/2012	Paid
10	10/03/2012	French	10	20/03/2012		LATE
11	10/05/2012	Kingsley	20	30/05/2012		LATE
12	10/06/2012	Fill	30	10/07/2012		LATE
13	10/06/2012	DentMark	10	20/06/2012		LATE

You will see that he only has to enter the date of the invoice, the terms and the date paid and his spreadsheet uses the IF function to automatically calculate if each invoice is paid, outstanding or late. This saves Ben a lot of time. If we look at his spreadsheet in formula view we can see how he has achieved this.

	A	B	C	D	E	F
1	Order Date	Customer	Terms	Due Date	Paid Date	Status
2	40911	Redbridge	30	=A2+C2	40970	=IF(E2="",IF(D2<TODAY(),"LATE","Outstanding"),"Paid")
3	40943	Cushington	30	=A3+C3	41007	=IF(E3="",IF(D3<TODAY(),"LATE","Outstanding"),"Paid")
4	40973	French	10	=A4+C4	41007	=IF(E4="",IF(D4<TODAY(),"LATE","Outstanding"),"Paid")
5	41339	Kingsley	30	=A5+C5	41003	=IF(E5="",IF(D5<TODAY(),"LATE","Outstanding"),"Paid")
6	40975	Fill	30	=A6+C6		=IF(E6="",IF(D6<TODAY(),"LATE","Outstanding"),"Paid")
7	40976	DentMark	10	=A7+C7	40996	=IF(E7="",IF(D7<TODAY(),"LATE","Outstanding"),"Paid")
8	40978	Redbridge	30	=A8+C8		=IF(E8="",IF(D8<TODAY(),"LATE","Outstanding"),"Paid")
9	40978	Cushington	30	=A9+C9	40985	=IF(E9="",IF(D9<TODAY(),"LATE","Outstanding"),"Paid")
10	40978	French	10	=A10+C10		=IF(E10="",IF(D10<TODAY(),"LATE","Outstanding"),"Paid")
11	41039	Kingsley	20	=A11+C11		=IF(E11="",IF(D11<TODAY(),"LATE","Outstanding"),"Paid")
12	41070	Fill	30	=A12+C12		=IF(E12="",IF(D12<TODAY(),"LATE","Outstanding"),"Paid")
13	41070	DentMark	10	=A13+C13		=IF(E13="",IF(D13<TODAY(),"LATE","Outstanding"),"Paid")

Ben's IF statement is very effective and efficient.

```
=IF(E3="",IF(D3<TODAY(),"LATE","Outstanding"),"Paid")
```

It is effective because it is looking at the date of the order, the due date and today's date. This is a clever use of his spreadsheet's today's date function (TODAY). His spreadsheet will automatically update itself according to today's date and say which invoices are late.

Other functions that Ben uses are:

Function	What it does
AVERAGE	Calculates the mean of a range of figures
MAX	Finds the biggest number
MIN	Finds the smallest number
MODE	Finds the most common item in a set of numbers or things

Searching and sorting data

Although spreadsheets are designed to work mainly with numbers, Ben's spreadsheet has text data as well. This means he can use his spreadsheet as a simple flat-file database. Although spreadsheets are

What you need to do ✓

If required, remember to select print areas for your spreadsheet before printing it:

- Think about what printed data you require.
- Select the correct view before printing.
- Consider whether you need landscape or portrait orientation.
- Preview before printing to check that you are printing what you require.
- You will need to experiment with your software to see how you can print selected data.
- Make sure that all data is fully displayed and can be read easily (columns are wide enough and cells deep enough).
- Do you need to produce a formula print?

not as easy to use as a specialised database package they are adequate for many of the simple tasks Ben has to perform. More importantly, the database functions in Ben's spreadsheet can be very useful in searching and sorting data.

Searching

Spreadsheets provide the ability to search the worksheet for any number, word, phrase or other text, letting the user scroll easily between search results.

Sorting

Ben's spreadsheet has a list of the dentists and their income. He can sort the data according to sex (M or F) and then according to income. He could also extract records from his data to calculate the average income of the dentists.

Printing from a spreadsheet

Ben decided to print his spreadsheet to give to the dentists. He spent a long time formatting the spreadsheet. His data was well organised and up to date. It looked good on screen so he decided to print out a hard copy, but when printed it looked awful and automatically printed the whole worksheet. This was quite annoying, as he only wanted to print part of the worksheet – the data on a specific number of pages.

Spreadsheet worksheets don't always look good on paper because they are not designed to fit on a typical printed page. They are designed to be as wide and long as the user needs them to be. This is ideal for editing and viewing on screen, but it means that data might not be a natural fit to a standard sheet of paper.

Ben knows that he should always view a print preview of a worksheet before he prints it out. By using print preview he can see exactly how his worksheet will look on the printed page.

In the print preview, Ben can even make certain changes, such as clicking on and dragging the print margins to make them wider or narrower.

Ben can print just the worksheet he is viewing by going to the print pane and selecting Print Active Sheets, or he can select Print Entire Workbook to print the whole file. It is also possible for him to tell the spreadsheet software how much of the worksheet to print and how to print it.

Ben simply highlights the cells that he wants to print by clicking the first cell in the range and dragging until he has highlighted all the cells that he wants to print. He can then print a small segment of his data by choosing Print Selection in the print options. Some software will also allow you to set the selection as Set Print Area so that the selected cells are remembered and whenever the spreadsheet is printed it will print only the selected area until the print area is cleared.

Other spreadsheet programs will allow you to set the print option to only print areas of the spreadsheet that contain data.

Protecting cells

When you are working on a spreadsheet you may want to protect or lock some of the cells or the whole spreadsheet. The purpose of locking cells is to prevent anyone using the spreadsheet, including yourself, from changing the contents of the protected cells. You might do this when sharing a spreadsheet with another person, or to protect some of the cells in a spreadsheet you are working on so you do not accidentally change content you do not want to change.

Charts and graphs

As you saw earlier Naomi has to turn her ice cream spreadsheet calculations into graphs and charts for inclusion in the newsletter. First she must choose the best type of chart to display the data. Good data presentation skills are important. Poor graphs and tables often lead both readers and writers to draw wrong conclusions from the data.

Naomi knows that there are some simple rules to follow:

- Simple is always better.
- Graphs, tables and charts can be used together.
- Use clear titles and labels.
- Provide a description of the main points.
- Don't compare variables with different scales.

Checking data

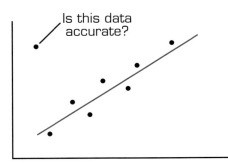

Naomi knows that accurate data is needed for all charts and graphs. If her data is weak or inaccurate, her graph will be of no use. She verifies any data that does not seem to make sense.

Adding scales

Naomi uses appropriate scales on the axes to represent data values.

Labelling axes

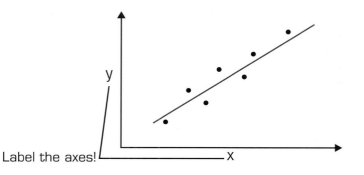

Label the axes!

Without labels or any explanation, the axes are just decoration. Naomi labels her axes so that readers know what scale points are plotted. Without axes labels she knows that the graph has no real value.

Descriptions

She can provide explanations in a variety of ways, but the most common is by providing a legend, directly labelling shapes or describing her graphic in a lead-in paragraph.

Including units

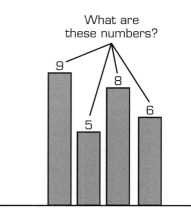

What are these numbers?

Naomi also knows that a chart or graph must show the units being used or it will not make any sense to the reader. Without a scale, data could mean anything from a percentage, a volume, or the number of people that drive a particular brand of car. She wants to eliminate the need for any guesswork.

Include sources

Naomi always includes where the data is sourced from. This does a couple of things. First, it makes your graph more reputable, and second, it allows people to check the data.

Line graphs

Line graphs are used to track changes over short and long periods of time. The y-axis represents frequency; the x-axis represents time or an interval of time. When smaller changes exist, line graphs are better to use than bar graphs. Line graphs can also be used to compare changes over the same period of time for more than one group. Naomi likes to use different colours or patterned lines to represent different groups. She has drawn this graph from the data she collected on milkshake sales, shown on page 177.

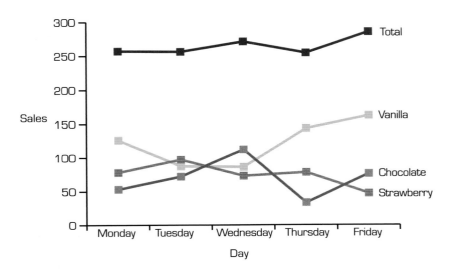

Key word

Curve fitting functionality

Line graphs consist of straight lines connecting 'real' data points. Some spreadsheet programs have **curve fitting functionality** to represent the functional relation between data points.

- Use a line graph:
  - ➤ if the x-axis requires an interval scale
  - ➤ to compare different graphs
  - ➤ to display interactions over two levels on the x-axis
  - ➤ to display long data rows
  - ➤ to find and compare changes over time
  - ➤ to forecast data values
  - ➤ to recognise comparisons between values
  - ➤ when it defines meaningful patterns (for example, a zigzag line).
- Do not use a line graph if the x-axis has non-numeric values.

Adding titles and labels to both axes of a graph is good practice.

Pie charts

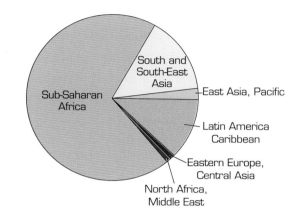

Pie charts are best to use when you are trying to compare parts of a whole. They do not show changes over time. This is a circular (360°) graphic representation of data. It compares subgroups or groups to the whole group or category using differently coloured or patterned segments.

Individual segments may be pulled out of the pie for emphasis (an 'exploded' pie chart).

Bar charts

Bar charts are used to compare things between different groups or to track changes over time. However, when trying to measure change over time, bar charts are best when the changes are quite large. Do not use bar charts for large data sets – use line graphs instead.

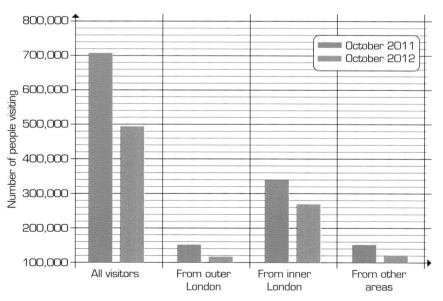

Scatter graphs

Scatter graphs are used to determine relationships between two different variables. The x-axis is used to measure one event (or variable) and the y-axis is used to measure the other. If both variables increase at the same time, they have a positive relationship. If one variable decreases while the other increases, they have a negative relationship. Sometimes the variables don't follow any pattern and have no relationship.

7

Types of business software databases

What you will learn

Database skills:
- When to use a database rather than a spreadsheet
- The difference between data, fields and records
- How to enter data into a database
- How to import data into a database
- Searching techniques, queries and reports

Using databases

Naomi Johnson at the SaverShop supermarket has built up quite a lot of suppliers and has collected names, addresses, telephone numbers and email addresses of them all.

Rather than search through pieces of paper every time the details of a supplier are needed, it makes sense to store this information electronically so that it is easier to contact one or other of them.

Whilst Naomi knows that she can sort and search for data in her spreadsheet she knows that databases have additional functionality such as the ability to create complex queries that can be saved and complex reports that format the data in a variety of ways. Using a database she also has the ability to easily create well-laid-out forms for data entry.

Naomi chooses a database for the following reasons:

- The information the company is storing is large and would be unmanageable in a spreadsheet.
- She needs to maintain records for ongoing use.
- She wants to generate saved reports based on the information stored.

Unlike her ice cream data that only has a few records, the company's supplier data has more than 2000 records. A database lets her open the data to multiple users, manage a large set of data and control how other users are going to enter the data.

Naomi also uses the company database to keep a record of all staff details. The company uses a database to organise information for easy retrieval. Data can be retrieved by asking questions of the data, called querying or searching, by sorting and filtering, and can be presented using a formatted report. Naomi can use a formatted report to produce an invoice, which can then be printed. Databases also involve the use of records to structure the tables. A record can contain any number of fields.

There are many different reasons why companies would use a database – the accuracy of the data and its correct manipulation are most important for the right results. In most cases, using the combination of a database to store business records and a spreadsheet to analyse selected information works best.

A spreadsheet can have serious drawbacks when used for large data storage and it is difficult to retrieve data from complex queries. Spreadsheets have little or no protection against data corruption from well meaning but poorly trained users. Naomi once created a large spreadsheet of suppliers that one of the other members of staff sorted by last name and saved the document. Unfortunately they had not selected any of the other columns and had not noticed the error before saving it, destroying all of her hard work.

False dates such as 31 April or 30 February cause problems in a spreadsheet but are automatically validated in a database. The food product number 0062 would get changed by a spreadsheet to 62 and the quantity 3/14 would get changed to 14 March unless she formatted the cells as text only which would prevent her using those cells for calculations. Naomi knows that these problems would not happen in a database.

Databases range from very simple to very complex. There are two main types of database programs. At the simple end there are 'flat-file' databases – also called single-file or list managers. Small businesses and large organisations use databases to add, edit, delete and search for information.

Database import and export formats are a little more complex than spreadsheets. The most common formats are:

Extension	Description
CSV	Each row is imported or exported as plain text, with commas used to separate data. The term CSV stands for comma separated values.
HTML	Each row is exported with HTML coding to form an HTML table that can be opened in a web browser or incorporated into a larger HTML page.
XML	Each row in the table is imported or exported with an identifying <Row> and each column is identified by an element that matches the column name.

Data, fields and records

Databases are divided into three main parts: data, fields and records.

Data

Databases are specially designed to organise data – data is therefore the key part of a database. Data can be in the form of pictures, text, numeric values, media or audio samples. Any information that you gather can be considered data. Here is an example of a database that we are all familiar with – an address book.

Name	Address	Phone Number	Email
Smooth, John	255 Main St	08973 456778	jsmooth@aol.com
Smith, Matthew	43 First Ave	06734 234567	matts@yahoo.com
Engles, Emily	2 Meadow Road	09782 346787	emilye@toms.com
Framly, Mary	43 Roxam Drive	06703 344567	mframly@bongo.com

All of the names, addresses, phone numbers, and email addresses are called data.

Fields

Fields are where the data goes when it is entered into a database. Look at the address book above. Each of the columns would be called a field. The words in bold are called Field Names, because they describe the information that is to be contained in the field. The 'Name' field contains the names of people, while the 'Address' field contains their addresses. Some fields can contain text; some, such as the 'Phone Number' field contain numeric values but are nearly always stored as text fields so that they retain the preceding zero and space after the area code. Other fields are also important such as date and logic fields.

Data type	Example	Description
Logic	Yes/No	The data can have only two possible opposing states such as yes or no, true or false, male or female. Sometimes displayed as a tick box.
Currency	£12.50	Denotes monetary value.
Date/Time	04/10/06 12:23:09	Any time or date. The way the time or date is displayed depends on how it is formatted.
Number (integer)	17	An integer is a whole number (positive or negative but no decimals).
Number (real)	23.67	A real number is any number including whole numbers and decimals. The software you are using will let you decide how many decimal places to use.
Text or string	John Smith	Generally letters but could also contain numbers and punctuation.

You can control the type of data that can be placed in a certain field. 'Validation' rules restrict the kind of data that is placed in the field. There are validation rules for text only and others for numeric or other data.

You can also limit the number of characters that you can place in a field to a maximum of your choice.

There is a type of rule that is called 'required, optional, or calculated':

■ **Required** means that the field is mandatory – that you must put data in the field. You cannot leave it empty.

■ **Optional** means the field does not have to be filled in.

What you need to do ☑

Make sure that you fully understand that databases must be:

- created
- formatted to show data in the most appropriate way.

Databases must be appropriate to the needs of the business:

- Are the field types suitable for the data?
- Is the field an appropriate length?
- Has the data from the csv file been imported correctly into the database table?
- Is the data appropriate to the needs of the business?

- **Calculated** means that the computer will fill in this field later after it has performed the necessary calculations.

When importing a csv file the database program suggests the most appropriate data type for each field. You should check this to make sure it is correct for the data contained in that field.

When setting up a database, making sure that data entry form boxes are large enough for the intended data, display all the data well and do not truncate any fields is vitally important.

Records

A record is a row of entered data. A database contains a list of records, each of which consists of fields. For example: Date of Birth, First Name, Initials, Last Name, Postcode, Phone Number and Email.

Importing data

Data may be in a different format such as a text file. To enter the data into a database you may need to import it. This is quite easy as the software should do most of the work for you.

Data types and formats

Using the correct data types for fields is very important – if it is not set up correctly then errors may occur when importing and entering your data. Some examples of field types are Date/Time, Currency, Numeric, Text, Yes/No. For each field type you may also choose what format you would like it in. For example, the Text field could be set to upper case or lower case.

Sorting and filtering data

Data is not always in the order in which we would like it to appear. It can be sorted as 'ascending' (lowest values are at the top of the column, or A–Z) or 'descending' (highest values are at the top of the column, or Z–A).

We can also filter data so that only certain information is visible. For example, people with a surname beginning with D, or between the ages of 20–25.

Advantages of databases

Databases are very useful for organising a collection of data or information. Here are some advantages of using a computerised database:

- Records need only be entered once but we can search and sort information in many different ways.

- We can sort data alphabetically, numerically or even by date. We can even sort particular data in search results.
- Searching for data can be very quick, even if the database contains a huge amount of data.
- Lots of data can be stored on easily transportable external devices.
- If data is lost we can easily retrieve it as long as we make regular backups.

Naomi can generate useful reports that can be customised. A report allows her to sort and summarise information that can then be printed out.

This is useful for meetings where she needs a paper copy to show people her findings. She can customise the presentation of her printed report to make it look really professional. Using the Report Wizard she can create a report of the shop's suppliers.

Working with a database

Naomi is always having to update the staff database. For example:

- Her boss has asked her to print out the staff list in alphabetical order by surname.
- The shop is busier than expected and two new members of staff have been recruited, whose details need adding to the database.
- It is necessary to record the National Insurance numbers of all staff. She has to add a new field to the database and enter the details from the data files.
- One member of staff is having difficulties with childcare arrangements and has had to hand their resignation in. Naomi has to delete their details from the database.
- One member of staff has moved house and she needs to update their contact details in the database.
- Lastly she is asked to print out a list of all female members of staff and a list of all staff under age 25, with the youngest at the top of the list.

Naomi knows that when she adds data to the existing database, it will follow the existing format set in the database, but she must enter the new details into the correct fields using the correct case. This ensures consistency across the shop's data – which is really important – it also makes it easier for her to view and change the data if needed later. Tables are the basic building blocks of a database. They are made up of records (sometimes called rows) and fields (sometimes called columns). Naomi uses Microsoft Access and she knows that it will automatically set the Format property for some new fields according to what she

hat you need to do ☑

tabase development skills:
mport data from a csv file.
Sort the data (change the order to
suit needs).
Enter, edit and format data.
Create queries:
  ► Sort data in a query.
Create reports.

types in. For example, if she enters 11:30a.m., Access sets the data type to Date/Time for the UK where she is based.

Naomi also uses auto inserts such as an automatic increment of the staff database number. Auto-increment fields are often used as a primary key in a table or as part of the primary key as they are unique.

Data in a database

SaverShop also has a supplier database.

The current information has been recorded using a spreadsheet. Naomi thinks that a database would be much better as there are a large number of entries and it would allow her to do a lot more with the data – such as better sorting, filtering and searching for information quickly. It could also have a user-friendly input form for her and other staff to update details.

Some of the types of data Naomi uses are text, number, currency and dates. When recording data in both spreadsheets and databases she has to decide what type of data is being recorded so that the software can deal with it appropriately and present it properly. The cells containing that data have to be formatted using the software.

Dates are often displayed in the YYYY–MM–DD format. Although this is not how we normally write down dates – for a computer it makes more sense. Many companies use this format at the start of their file names too, for example a document produced on 4 February 2012 would be stored with the first part of the filename as 20120204. The computer will then automatically list the files in date order. However, if they put the day first, files from a range of years and months would be listed together making it hard to find the latest file without sorting.

Having entered the data into the database Naomi is asked to amend the data.

The owner of the supermarket has decided to use suppliers from the United Kingdom only, so Naomi needs to delete any suppliers outside of the United Kingdom.

She also needs to query the data for suppliers of fresh fruit and vegetables and print out suppliers' names and phone numbers only.

All of the case study businesses use databases. Here is an example of a database Dihana created for the Eye Planet cinema showing the names and details of people who are 'Planeteer' members and what level of membership they have.

Person Code	Surname	Forename	DoB	Gender	Planeteer Membership
1470	Bains	Stephen	27/07/1991	M	Junior
1683	Thomson	Scott	11/03/1991	M	Basic
1788	Jones	Callum	05/12/1990	M	Silver
1839	Ahmed	Saleem	30/07/1991	M	Basic
1915	Saleh	Abdi	25/10/1991	M	Basic
1922	Lu	Chian	19/04/1990	M	Junior
1965	Jameson	Lauren	01/08/1991	F	Gold
1976	Moore	Charlotte	26/05/1990	F	Platinum

Below is the data entry form for inputting new members' details or for the purpose of editing existing members' records.

Members

Person Code	1922
Surname	Lu
Forename	Chian
DoB	19/04/1990
Gender	M
Planeteer Membership	Junior

Each of the fields are formatted for the specific data that will be inputted. For example, the 'Person Code' field has been formatted to accept only integer data. That means that only whole numbers will be accepted into that field – it won't accept letters or decimal numbers.

The 'Surname', 'Forename' and 'Planeteer Membership' fields have been formatted to accept only text as obviously names of people and the types of memberships do not contain numbers.

The 'DoB' (or Date of Birth) field is formatted to accept a date. However, further formatting is required in this field to inform the database of what format to accept the date in, that is 'dd/mm/yyyy' format, 'day month year' or some other date format.

Finally, the 'Gender' field is in logic format, accepting only 'M' for male of 'F' for female.

Queries

Queries are methods of interrogating and manipulating data within database tables by creating a set of 'rules' that filter the specific information required. For example, in the database above, you could construct a query to investigate which male members have a 'basic' Planeteer membership or which female members were born in 1991.

As Dihana uses Microsoft Access, the easiest way to construct a query is to use a 'Query Wizard'. This tool allows the selection of specific fields and the application of user-created 'rules' to those fields to discover the information required. Dihana could also have done this in Design View.

Searching databases

The Cushington Ceramic Seal Company has to share data across a range of suppliers. They therefore use an online database. It works exactly the same as an offline database and Greg Hanson uses a search form he fills in. He can conduct a simple search or a complex search.

Simple search

A unique identifier is a number that is completely exclusive to that record and cannot be duplicated for another record. Greg can enter the unique identifier in a single search field, which takes him directly to the record he is looking for.

The main search screen usually appears when you open the application. Greg then has to enter some search criteria before he can access anything within the application. Once on the main search screen, he can enter the unique identifier into the relevant search field, and then clicking 'Search' will bring up the matching record.

Complex search

More complex searches work on the same principle as a simple search. When Greg does not know the reference, he can use a variety of other criteria such as postcode, surname, etc. For example, when Greg is searching for members born between two dates.

To narrow down a search Greg can use more than one field. For example, if he knows that a Mr Taylor lives in the area of Oxbridge he can enter these into the relevant search fields. This produces a list of all the people with the surname 'Taylor' who live in the 'Oxbridge' area.

Greg can also sort within a search. This means that once he has performed the search he sorts the data so that it is more useful to him, for example by name.

7

Operators

Searches use commands – or 'operators' – to limit the number of potential hits and increase the likelihood that those hits are useful. The most commonly used operators are AND, OR and NOT. They are sometimes, but not always, case sensitive, so always enter them in capital letters. The criteria will need to be entered into the search box for the particular field that is being queried.

AND will give hits only if the data contains both/all words, but remember that entering 'Male AND Female' will not return any results as you will not have data that suggests anyone is both male and female! OR will result in hits containing either word, it doesn't matter which.

NOT can bring up all records except those that contain the search criteria, but can also be used for records that have the first word/phrase but not the second word.

Greg can search a database in many ways. One way of searching is to use AND, OR and NOT. Other ways of searching include using the operators >, >=, <, <=, <> and =. For example:

What are you searching for?	Example	Operator
Must be greater than 10	>10	>
Must be greater than or exactly equal to 10	>= 10	>=
Must be less than 5	<5	<
Must be less than or exactly equal to 5	<= 5	<=
Must be between 1 and 4	>0 AND <5	AND
Must be red or blue	red OR blue	OR
Must not be 50	NOT 50	NOT
Must not be Z	<> Z	<>
Z is the only entry that can be returned	=Z	=

As Greg uses Microsoft Access he can also use the 'BETWEEN… AND' operator. This determines whether the value of an expression falls within a specified range of values.

Reports

A report can be made from data in a whole database table or a query that you have run. The easiest way to do this would be to use the Report Wizard and follow the steps through.

You should include the relevant fields, decide how you would like to lay out your report and what style it will have, then simply click finish to preview your report.

This is an example of the Report Wizard Dihana uses:

Report Wizard

Which fields do you want on your report?

You can choose from more than one table or query.

Tables/Queries

Table: Members

Available Fields:

Person Code
Surname
Forename
DoB
Gender
Planeteer Membership

Selected Fields:

Cancel | < Back | Next > | Finish

Producing forms and printing reports

When you create data-entry forms or when you print reports you need to think about keeping things consistent, decide upon the style and layout for the display and the appearance of paper-based reports that users are going to see. The layout will depend on the purpose of the data – you would not use the same display for labels and a grouped tabular report.

Grouped reports

Information is often more informative when viewed by group. For instance, a report that groups sales by region can highlight trends that otherwise might go unnoticed.

Text

Format text in reports (style, colour, size, font). Decide upon a format that you like, looks good and is user friendly. Practise using different formatting techniques but remember to keep it consistent.

Orientation

Information in a table can be presented in landscape or portrait format. Which looks better? Which displays the data more clearly? Is all the required data shown in full?

Colour

The use of colour can make reports look much more attractive. Try using different background and fill colours to see what works best.

Greg at Cushington Ceramic Seals generates three types of reports: columnar, tabular and group.

Customer	
Company	AAS
First name	HASIB
Surname	RAHMAN
Sex	M
Ethnic group	BN
Email address	hasib.rahman@email.net
Job	Rep
Company	AAS
First name	ZAMAN
Surname	ALI
Sex	F
Ethnic group	ABP
Email address	zaman.ali@email.net
Job	Director

Columnar report

Accountants				
Job	First name	Surname	Email address	Company
Accounts	BEVERLEY	MORRISON	beverley.morrison@email.net	Cosmic
Accounts	MARJANI	AMISI	marjani.amisi@email.net	Cobalt Engineering
Accounts	EFRA	ACQUAYE	efra.acquaye@email.net	AAS
Accounts	SARAH	WHITE	sarah.white@email.net	Cobalt Engineering
Accounts	IMRAN	QAZI	imran.qazi@email.net	GoSoft
Accounts	CHLOE	CLARK	chloe.clark@email.net	Ceramic Glues
Accounts	IBRAR	QAZI	ibrar.qazi@email.net	Temple Tools
Accounts	LOUISE	HUNT	louise.hunt@email.net	Ceramic Glues
Accounts	ZAINAB	CLARK	zainab.clark@email.net	Temple Tools
Accounts	SATOKI	WATANABE	satoki.watanabe@email.net	GoSoft
Accounts	ALEX	BURNS	alex.burns@email.net	GoSoft
Accounts	SHAZIA	KHAN	shazia.khan@email.net	Timkin
Accounts	EVAN	GEORGE	evan.george@email.net	Diamond Cutters
Accounts	HASSAN	SAEED	hassan.saeed@email.net	Cosmic
Accounts	FIAM	IQBAL	fiam.iqbal@email.net	Cobalt Engineering
Accounts	TIA	COLLINS	tia.collins@email.net	Cobalt Engineering
Accounts	MAHEK	AHMED	mahek.ahmed@email.net	Diamond Cutters
Accounts	RIFAT	GAZI	rifat.gazi@email.net	Temple Tools

Tabular report

Greg knows that information is often easier to understand when it is divided into groups. For example, a report that groups suppliers by region can highlight changes in the supply chain that otherwise might go unnoticed. Greg's company is based in a multi-ethnic community and the company is keen to track suppliers to ensure that they are truly reflecting their cultural heritage.

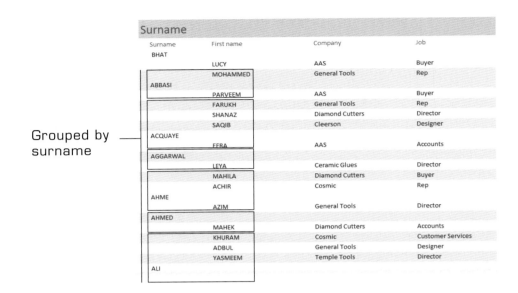

Grouped by surname

Surname	First name	Company	Job
BHAT			
	LUCY	AAS	Buyer
	MOHAMMED	General Tools	Rep
ABBASI			
	PARVEEM	AAS	Buyer
	FARUKH	General Tools	Rep
	SHANAZ	Diamond Cutters	Director
	SAQIB	Cleerson	Designer
ACQUAYE			
	EFRA	AAS	Accounts
AGGARWAL			
	LEYA	Ceramic Glues	Director
	MAHILA	Diamond Cutters	Buyer
	ACHIR	Cosmic	Rep
AHME			
	AZIM	General Tools	Director
AHMED			
	MAHEK	Diamond Cutters	Accounts
	KHURAM	Cosmic	Customer Services
	ADBUL	General Tools	Designer
	YASMEEM	Temple Tools	Director
ALI			

Group report

8

Design considerations

Ria Mathews works at the leisure centre. She studied graphic design at college. Ria knows that ensuring consistency of design across all communications to customers is very important to business. The leisure centre spends large amounts of money to make certain that they have a good image that is suited to their customers.

The name given to this is house style. It is important to ensure that all business documents – from electronic documents such as websites, to spreadsheets, formal letters and advertising materials have the same look and feel.

Colour

Ria knows the importance of colour in design.

Whilst Ria knows that using colour can be very effective – how much colour and what types of colour used is very important. She does not want to overwhelm the viewer by using all kinds of colours. Instead, specific colours are chosen to highlight the leisure centre's best aspects and she uses those colours sparingly, with the focus on emphasising the impact parts of her designs.

Ria knows that certain colours, such as some yellows and pinks, are very difficult to see and read. Text and background colours should complement or contrast with each other.

Colour checklist

- Do on-screen colours look as you expected when printed?
- Do the colours work together – does the information stand out from the background?
- Have you stuck to a sensible number of colours?

Images

Ria also chooses images with care so that they illustrate or support the text. She knows that backgrounds do not have to be white – they can be coloured, shaded or even contain a secondary image printed faintly to cover some unused white space.

Make sure that you fully understand design elements and apply these to all your documents:

- Design a common house style for all the needs of the business.
- Choose layout, colour and text to suit the business needs of your task and the audience.
- Remember your task relates to a business.
- Use the tools and facilities in the software application to improve your document.
- Where appropriate use automatic fields, headers and footers.

Check your work carefully to ensure the layout is consistent.

Hints and tips

Remember to keep in mind at all times the purpose and intended audience for your documents. Your document should attract the right people and to do this think about the layout and formatting you use. For example, if you were creating a poster about healthy eating aimed at 5–7 year olds then you could use a font such as comic sans (blue, size 18pt), with limited text and more images, which could be big, bright and funny.

Image checklist
● Does your choice of image help to get your message across?   ● Have you considered copyright if using images taken from secondary sources?   ● Have you resized the image correctly so that it has the same proportions or shape as the original?   ● Is the image in a position that will attract attention?   ● Is the image suitable for your audience?

Layout

One of the most important elements Ria has to consider is layout.

Ria has to arrange her pages and everything that goes on them so that it is fit for purpose. This includes text and images (known as elements).

Layout checklist
● Are the text and images in sensible positions and grouped together if they need to be?   ● Have you aligned the text so that it is easy to read?   ● Have you made good use of the full page area, and placed your images and text appropriately, for example within margins?   ● Is the layout consistent?

Consistency and house style

Most businesses achieve consistency by having what is called a style guide or house style. The style guide states what colours, type face and point sizes must be used in all documentation and even how to spell certain words. It may sound strange but words such as internet can also be spelled correctly as Internet with a capital 'I'. Whilst both are correct, having inconsistency (using both) gives a bad impression to a customer.

Whilst you do not need to go as far as having a style guide for your own work, you must ensure you use a common house style when you produce materials for a business.

There are lots of different ways to make documents look more interesting – by organising text and images so that they are well presented, and by formatting documents, for example to make particular points stand out. Using tables is a good way of organising information in a document. In some cases, presenting information as a chart or graph makes it easier for the audience to understand.

Breaking up text and images into paragraphs, and adding line breaks and page breaks make documents a lot easier to follow. But make sure that line breaks, page breaks and spacing are consistent throughout any document you produce.

Other design elements

Orientation

You have a choice of using portrait or landscape orientation – this refers to the way your page will print. Most applications are set up by default to portrait orientation.

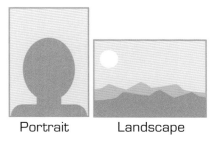

Portrait   Landscape

Margins

Margins refer to the white space around the edge of a document. You can make the margins smaller so that you can fit more on to the page.

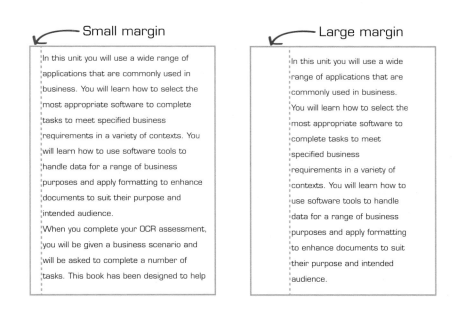

Small margin

In this unit you will use a wide range of applications that are commonly used in business. You will learn how to select the most appropriate software to complete tasks to meet specified business requirements in a variety of contexts. You will learn how to use software tools to handle data for a range of business purposes and apply formatting to enhance documents to suit their purpose and intended audience.
When you complete your OCR assessment, you will be given a business scenario and will be asked to complete a number of tasks. This book has been designed to help

Large margin

In this unit you will use a wide range of applications that are commonly used in business. You will learn how to select the most appropriate software to complete tasks to meet specified business requirements in a variety of contexts. You will learn how to use software tools to handle data for a range of business purposes and apply formatting to enhance documents to suit their purpose and intended audience.

Columns

A column is one or more vertical blocks of text/images positioned on a page and separated by gutters. Columns are used to make large amounts of text easier to read. For example, newspapers use them to separate different stories and break up large amounts of text in long stories.

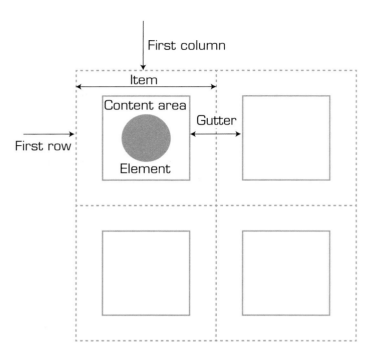

You can add columns to a document but then have to work out what gutter space you need between columns.

Text wrapping

Text wrapping is a feature supported by many word processing and other software packages to enable you to surround a picture or diagram with text. The text wraps around the graphic.

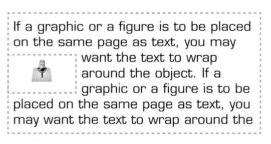

If a graphic or a figure is to be placed on the same page as text, you may want the text to wrap around the object. If a graphic or a figure is to be placed on the same page as text, you may want the text to wrap around the

Text justification

Text can also be justified. For example:

`Left`

`Right`

`Centred`

Text can even be fully justified where the text is justified to both the left and right margins, but this can lead to strange word spacing.

Headers, footers and page numbering

It is good practice to get used to using headers, footers and page numbering – particularly footers and page numbering. Imagine if you produced a ten-page document which did not have page numbers, then printed it, dropped the pages and had to figure out which order the pages went in. It is also good practice to put in the footer some information that identifies the author (who produced the document) and where the document is stored. For example:

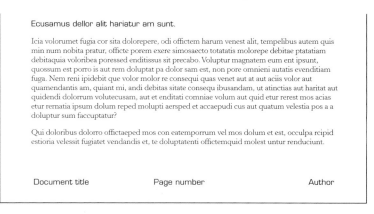

Page breaks

If you are using more than one page for your document, in most applications you will find that the application continues automatically onto the next page as you add more material. But this may be at an inappropriate point, for example leaving only one line of a paragraph on the previous page or a subheading at the bottom of the page with no following text. You can decide where is the best place to end one page and start the next by adding a page break.

Widows and orphans

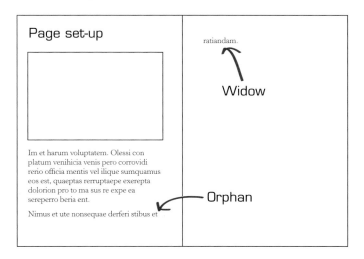

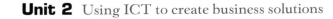

You need to be careful not to make it hard for the reader by having widows and orphans. A widow is the short last line of a paragraph at the top of a page. An orphan is the first line of a paragraph or a heading at the foot of a page. Headings/subheadings should have at least two lines of following text.

Formatting text

Formatting text means changing its appearance. There are many editing tools and techniques that are available to help you design and structure your document so that it is fit for purpose. Most of these tools are available on the tool bar. In most software applications the formatting toolbar is very similar – once you have mastered the facilities in one package you can apply the same skills in other software.

Font style

The text in a document is styled in a type of font. Examples of popular fonts include: Times New Roman, Courier New, Arial, Calibri, Apple Chancery, Baskerville Old Face and Century Gothic.

Font size

Font size is a measurement of the size of type. Font size is measured in points (pt). Font sizes in Microsoft Word, for example, range from small (8pt) to very large (72pt).

Select appropriate font sizes throughout your document. Headings, for example, should be in a larger font size than the main text. If you choose a very small font size, some people will have difficulty reading the text. If you choose a large font size then you may not be able to fit as much text on the page as intended.

The most important thing to remember when considering font style and size is that you pick an appropriate font style and size for the document you are producing. For example, a business report would be best presented in one of the traditional fonts such as Arial 11pt, whereas a poster advertising a Halloween party could use Chiller 24pt.

Text style

You may want different sections of your document to stand out, for example headings or important points. To do this you can choose styles such as **bold**, *italic* and <u>underlined</u> to emphasise the selected text. However, if text needs to be emphasised in the body of the document, underlining should be avoided as it could be interpreted as a weblink and could cause confusion to the reader.

Text colour

You can select different colours to emphasise text. Be careful when using colour on business documents as inappropriate or random use of coloured text may make your document look unprofessional or make it difficult to read.

Text spacing

You can also adjust the line spacing between the lines in each paragraph. The default is usually single line spacing but if you want to spread it out more you can choose 1.5 or double line spacing. To make good use of the available space, most packages will allow you to adjust the spacing in much smaller increments.

There should be no space before punctuation marks. Modern convention is to have one space after punctuation, however some organisations still require there to be two spaces after full stops, question marks and exclamation marks. Either one or two spaces are acceptable but they must be consistently applied throughout the document. There should be no spaces before or after a hyphen (for example, part-time), but a dash – sometimes used to separate phrases, should have one space either side.

Indents

There are four types of indents: left indent, right indent, first line indent and hanging indent.

Left and right indents control the space between the text and the left or right margin and are often set using a ruler.

The first line indent is used to indent the first line of a paragraph, similar to how you might use a tab.

Block indenting is often used to identify a quote in text.

Tabs

Tabs are a formatting feature used to align text. When you press the Tab key, the software inserts a tab character and moves the text or number insertion point to the next tab setting, called a tab stop.

Bullets and numbering

Bulleted or numbered lists can make a list of points easier to read if used appropriately. When deciding whether to use bullets or numbers, consider whether the target audience is supposed to read the points in a certain order. If so, use a numbered list.

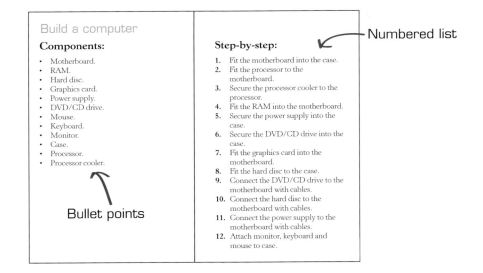

Build a computer

Components:

- Motherboard.
- RAM.
- Hard disc.
- Graphics card.
- Power supply.
- DVD/CD drive.
- Mouse.
- Keyboard.
- Monitor.
- Case.
- Processor.
- Processor cooler.

Bullet points

Numbered list

Step-by-step:

1. Fit the motherboard into the case.
2. Fit the processor to the motherboard.
3. Secure the processor cooler to the processor.
4. Fit the RAM into the motherboard.
5. Secure the power supply into the case.
6. Secure the DVD/CD drive into the case.
7. Fit the graphics card into the motherboard.
8. Fit the hard disc to the case.
9. Connect the DVD/CD drive to the motherboard with cables.
10. Connect the hard disc to the motherboard with cables.
11. Connect the power supply to the motherboard with cables.
12. Attach monitor, keyboard and mouse to case.

Tables

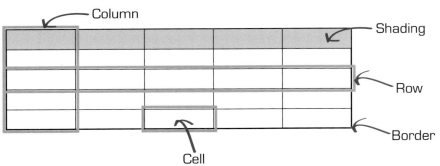

Column — Shading — Row — Border — Cell

Sometimes using tables to display information in a document can make it look better and clearer for the target audience to see and understand.

Tables are made up of rows, columns and cells, as shown in the example above. The lines and the shaded areas are called borders and shading. You can type and paste an image or block of text into the cells. As you type into a cell, in most word processors, it will expand to take all the text. However, if you wish to apply text wrap in a spreadsheet you will probably need to select this option.

Automatic fields

Some information, such as dates and times can be inserted automatically into documents. The date or time can be set to update each time the document its opened ensuring that the document automatically records its last update. The code which displays the date or time is called a field. There is a wide range of fields that can be inserted:

- Date/time fields:
  - creation date

- last saved date
- when it was printed
- Author
- File name/size
- Number of pages/words.

Images

An image can be used to illustrate text, as a logo or decoration. Be very careful about the use of images in business documents. Always ask yourself whether the image is necessary and whether it adds to the meaning.

Charts

Charts or graphs can be created within a wide range of software. They can be printed out as a single document or can be created, imported or embedded into a word processed, presentation, web page or DTP document. In all cases they must have a heading and be properly labelled.

Diagrams

Diagrams use basic shapes to represent objects, and to show how they relate to each other. When shapes and objects are used with text or other objects you should group them so that they remain together if/when they are moved or if data is added to the document.

White space

This is the space on a page (either a printed page or on screen, as in a web page) that has no text or images, even if the page is not white. Good use of white space can give a page a classic or elegant appearance. Expensive brands often use layouts with little text and a lot of white space. But poor and inconsistent use of white space can make a page appear incomplete.

Once you have read through your document, in practice tasks ask a friend to do the same thing and get their opinion.

Different types of software have different features that can be used to create different design features. Make sure you are familiar with the design features of the software you are using.

Hints and tips

Before you start, stop and consider who the audience is! Use an appropriate style for them when producing your document. When you have finished your document:
- Read through and check for accuracy and consistency.
- Check for spelling mistakes – use the spellchecker.
- Use any other checking facilities available in your software, for example grammar checker or design checker.
- Check you have included everything you needed to – is it complete?
- Ask yourself, is your content, including images, sound, text, video and anything else you have included, fit for purpose?
- Read through your text – is it interesting and will people understand the points you are making?

Look through your document and ask yourself these questions:
- How do the colours used in the document, spreadsheet or database look when printed?
- Can the text be clearly read?
- Are any logos and images positioned correctly, is the quality good?
- Does the information in the document fulfil its purpose?

Hints and tips

Remember house style and make effective use of formatting tools. Whichever software application you choose, apply your designs consistently. Appropriate formatting of all of your documents, including word processed and DTP documents, presentations, spreadsheets and databases will be taken into consideration when awarding you marks. It will be up to you to select the most suitable document type and software to use for each task and to apply appropriate formatting to ensure that each document is fit for purpose and appropriate for the target audience.

Glossary

Absolute cell referencing: You can set a cell reference to be an absolute cell reference when you want it to stay fixed on a specific cell and not to change when it is cut and pasted into a new position. 181

Access rights: Control who has access to a computer system, folders or files. 60

Address book: Where all email addresses and other contact details such as mobile phone numbers can be stored. 83

Adware (Advertising-supported software): A software package that automatically shows adverts, such as a pop-up. 111

Analogue to digital converter: A device that changes analogue signals into digital signals. 48

Anti-virus software: Used to detect viruses and remove them to limit their damage and impact to the computer system. 113

Application: The software that allows a user to carry out a task on a computer system. 25

Archive: A copy of data that is not being used at the present time. Archives are not stored on the computer system but are kept safely away from the system. 67

Attachment: A file that is sent with an email. Attachments can be, for example, documents, presentations, sound or video files. 65

Backup: A copy of a file or data that is currently being used. A backup is stored away from the original file or data. 67

Bandwidth: A measure of the rate of data transfer, usually stated in bits per second. 31

Blind carbon copy (Bcc): A copy of an email sent to someone whose name and email address is not visible to other recipients. 82

Body (email): Where the actual content of the email is written. 81

Bulletin board: An information storage system designed to allow any authorised computer user to access, view and add to it remotely. 75

Carbon copy (Cc): Enables everyone who is sent an email to see who else was sent it. 82

Cell address: The reference ID for each cell. For example, A1 – column A, row 1; E25 – column E, row 25. 178

Cell range: A group of cells in a specific area. For example, A1:C10 contains all the cells in the grid from A1 to C10. It includes A1 to A10, B1 to B10 and C1 to C10. 178

Chat room: A site on the internet where a number of users can communicate in real time about a particular topic. 74

Column: Goes vertically up and down. One cell wide by an infinite number of cells deep. For example, Column A, Column B. 178

Computer Misuse Act (CMA): The law that relates to illegal access to files and data stored on computer systems. It was introduced to cope with the increase in hacking and viruses. 100

Computer systems: The hardware, both internal components and peripherals, and the software that make up one or more computers. If there is more than one computer, then these must be connected and work together in some way to be called a 'system'. 5

Computer virus: A computer program that can replicate itself and spread from one computer to another. 110

Contact: An entry in an address book about a person. 20

Cookie: A text file that can be read using, for example, Notebook in the Microsoft Windows operating system. The file usually contains two pieces of information – a site name and unique user ID. 104

Creative Commons: A non-profit organisation that enables the sharing and use of creativity and knowledge through free legal tools. 166

Cultural: The behaviours and beliefs characteristic of a particular social, ethnic or age group. 123

Cyber bullying: When one person or a group of people try to threaten or embarrass someone else using digital technology. 103

Data: Raw numbers, letters or characters that have no meaning until processed. 42

Database: The data that is organised and managed by a database management system. The data is stored in a computer file consisting of fields and records. 39

Data capture forms: Paper or online forms used to collect data ready for entering into a computer system. 42

Data controller: The person who decides what data needs to be collected and what it will be used for and how. 97

Data encryption software: Software that is used to encrypt a file or data. 61, 114

Data Protection Act (DPA): The law that governs how collected data can be used by organisations and the actions that can be taken by data subjects if their data is abused.

Data security: The protection of computer data from accidental loss or unauthorised access. 25

Data subject: A person that data is being collected from or stored about. 97

Data user: Someone who needs to access or use data as part of their job. 97

Denial of service (DoS): An attempt to make a computer, website or network system unavailable to its users. 111

Desktop computer: A computer system consisting of a base unit to which other components such as a monitor, keyboard and mouse are attached separately. Desktop computers are not usually portable. 7

Diary management software (DMS): Enables users to organise work schedules by completing tasks such as creating appointments, meetings, tasks, projects, to-do lists, setting reminders and inviting participants. 85

Disk image: A complete copy of a hard disk. 70

Drop down menus: Menus that appear to drop down and present a set of choices to a user. 44

Editing cells: Changing the contents of cells in a spreadsheet. Changing the appearance of cells is formatting. 178

Electronic mail (Email): A way that a computer user connected to the internet (including those connected via mobile devices) can communicate with other connected users through text and send documents, images, sound and video clips as attachments. 74

Email etiquette (netiquette): Rules that should always be followed when sending emails. 83

Encryption code or key: A set of characters, a phrase or numbers that are used when encrypting or decrypting data or a file. 61

Ethernet: A technology for connecting computer systems and devices in a local network. 23

Exporting: The opposite of importing data. It means to format data so that it can be used by another application. The export function in a program creates a file in a format that another application understands (e.g. text or CSV), enabling the two programs to share the same data. 175

File format: The method of structuring data within a file for storing on a computer storage device. 55

Firewall: Used to help protect a computer system from threats and attacks. This is done by controlling what data can and cannot pass through it. Can be either hardware or software. 34

Flash memory: Computer memory that can be rewritten many times. Used in USB memory sticks, digital camera flash memory cards and solid state disks. 21

Glossary

Forum: An internet forum, or message board, is an online discussion site where people can hold conversations in the form of posted messages. 75

Graphical user interface (GUI): An interface to a computer system that uses images/graphics to represent choices, applications or navigation actions. 37

Hacker: A person who finds weaknesses in a computer system. 102

Hacking: A way of finding weaknesses in an established system and exploiting them. 100

Header (email): Part of an email that usually contains From, To, Subject, Date and Attachment information. 81

http: Hypertext transfer protocol used for transmitting web pages over the internet, for example. 62

https: A secure form of http used for transmitting personal data or bank details, for example. 62

Information: Processed data that has a meaning and is in context. 42

Information Commissioner: The person who enforces the Data Protection Act (DPA). 97

Instant messaging: The exchange of typed messages between computer users in real time via the internet. 8

Key logger: A piece of hardware or software that records the real-time activity of a computer user including the keyboard keys they press. 104

Mobile application (app): A software application that is usually designed to run on smartphones/tablet computers. 86

Mobile phone positioning: The obtaining of the current position of a mobile phone. 106

Network: A network connects computer systems and other devices together so that data can be exchanged. 22

Operating system: The software that manages the hardware and allows other software to run on a computer system. 25

Optical media: The media that are used by optical storage devices such as CD and DVD drives. Optical media include CDs, CD-Rs and CD-RWs, DVDs, DVD-Rs and DVD-RWs and BluRay disks. 21

Password: A set of characters known only to the user that provides security so that only the authorised user can gain access to a computer system. 34

Peer-to-peer: This is used to transfer files or data directly between computing devices over a network without the use of a server. 64

Permissions: A set of file attributes that determine what a user can do with a file, for example read, write, edit or delete a file. 60

Personal data: Facts and opinions about a living individual. 48

Phishing: A way of attempting to acquire personal information by pretending to be from a trustworthy source. 110

Portable computer: These are computer systems in which all the components and required peripherals are contained in a single case. They can run from battery power and so can be carried around and used in different places quite easily. 7

Processor: A computer chip, or chips, that is/are the hardware that carries out the instructions of a program in a computer system. 25

Radio buttons: Buttons that can be clicked to make an exclusive choice. 44

Radio frequency identification (RFID) tag: Small computing devices that use radio waves to transfer data from the tag to a computer system. 50

Relative: Something with a strong connection to another. 181

Relative cell referencing: A spreadsheet cell reference is relative by default. When a formula or function is copied and pasted to another cell, the cell references in the formula or function will change to reflect their new position in the spreadsheet. 181

Removable media: Storage media that can be removed from the computer system. Examples include CDs, DVDs, USB memory sticks and external hard disks. 69

Resolution: The number of pixels that are displayed in an image. 25

Row: Goes horizontally left to right. One cell deep by an infinite number of cells wide. For example, Row 1, Row 2. 178

Short message service (SMS): A system that lets mobile phone users send and receive text messages. 74

Social networking: The use of a dedicated website to communicate informally with other members of the site, by posting, for example, messages, photographs or videos. 12

Societal: Relating to human society and its members' normal practice in businesses and institutions, accepted behaviours and laws. 123

Spreadsheet: A software application that uses cells arranged in rows and columns to organise and manipulate data with formulae. 38

Spyware: A type of malware (malicious software) installed on a computer system that collects information about users without their knowledge. 83

Subject line: Provides information about the subject of the email. 82

SUM: A spreadsheet function that will add up a row or column of figures. 180

Trojan: A stand-alone malicious program designed to give full control of a computer infected with a Trojan to another computer. 110

Undo: This reverts to a previous state or 'undoes' an action. 132

USB: Universal Serial Bus used for the connection of devices such as printers or flash memory to computer systems. 21

User ID: Identifies a user to the computer system. 34

Videoconferencing: Allows people at two or more locations to communicate by simultaneous two-way video and audio transmissions. 76

Voice over Internet Protocol (VoIP): A system that allows the human voice (analogue signal) to be converted to digital so that telephone calls may be made over the internet. 75

Voice telephone: Enables people to talk to each other, holding a conversation. These can be fixed land line or mobile. 73

Webcam: A video camera that inputs to a computer connected to the internet, so that live streaming of images can be viewed by internet users. 29

Wireless access point (WAP): A device that allows computer systems or devices to connect wirelessly into an exisiting network. 24

Worm: A stand-alone computer program that replicates itself so it can spread to other computers. 110

Index